Maths

KEY STAGE 2
REVISION & PREPARATION

I think I'll start with 4 x 5...

4 x 9 x 5

Peter Patilla

Published by Letts Educational
The Chiswick Centre
414 Chiswick High Road
London W4 5TF
Telephone: 020 8996 3333
Fax: 020 8742 8390
E-mail: mail@lettsed.co.uk
Website: www.letts-education.com

Letts Educational is part of the Granada Learning Group. Granada Learning is a division of Granada plc.

First published 2003

ISBN 184085 9105

British Library Cataloguing in Publication Data
A catalogue record for this book is available from the British Library.

This book was designed and produced for Letts Educational by
Bridge Creative Services Limited, Bicester
Commissioned by Kate Newport
Project management by Phillipa Allum
Editing by Kearsey & Finn Limited, Cambridge
Cover design by Santamaria Design Consultants Ltd
Illustrations by John Plumb, Jan Simmonett
Production by PDQ
Printed and bound in Italy by G. Canale & C., Turin

CONTENTS

How do I use the pages to revise?

Each topic is shown across two pages and is set out in the same way. It will help you revise important facts, ideas and skills.

You have almost certainly come across all these ideas already in your mathematics lessons. Use the pages to remind yourself about them and to check your understanding.

To revise a topic:

◆ Read the page slowly and carefully. Give yourself time to think about the ideas.

◆ Make sure you understand what everything means. If there is something you don't understand, ask someone who can help you with it.

◆ If possible do the activity. It will help you check your understanding.

◆ Read through the page again a few days later. This will help you remember.

> **The left-hand introduction** explains what the topic is about and introduces the important facts and ideas that you will need to remember.

WRITTEN ADDITION AND SUBTRACTION

Most errors made when adding or subtracting are caused by careless mistakes. Setting your work out neatly and checking whether the answer seems sensible will help avoid careless mistakes.

- Line up the numbers when adding or subtracting.
- Check your calculation by another method.

With most calculations you will have to decide the most efficient method for you. What matters is that the answer you get is correct.

* Can I calculate these mentally?
* Will I have to work it out with pencil and paper?
* Should I use a calculator?

Line up the numbers correctly when adding or subtracting.

With whole numbers line up the units digits. Remember the order in which you add does not matter.

$$2457 + 26 + 156$$

```
  2457
   156
+   26
```

$$34\,652 - 6486$$

```
  34652
-  6486
```

With decimals line up the decimal point and make the number of decimal places the same.

$$12.34 + 0.7 + 3.575$$

```
 12.340
  3.575
+ 0.700
```

$$4.2 - 1.375$$

```
  4.200
- 1.375
```

Check addition by adding up in a different order.

Check subtraction by adding the answer to what has been taken away.

If you know this fact: $7456 + 897 = 8353$

you should be able to answer these three facts without any more working out:

$897 + 7456$ $8353 - 897$ $8353 - 7456$

> **REMEMBER**
> Adding zeros to the ends of a decimal does not alter its value.
> $0.4 = 0.40 = 0.400$

42

Talk about some different ways of subtracting 25.6 from 1205. Discuss how the answer can be checked.

> **The REMEMBER box** reminds you about a key point. Often it is something that many people get wrong or muddled.

The bullets give you the main ideas 'in a nutshell'.

Estimating and approximating

When adding and subtracting large numbers or decimals, estimate or approximate the answer to check whether the calculation seems sensible. It does not matter whether you estimate before the calculation or after – it is only a check.

Checks are particularly important if you are using a calculator because it is so easy to enter a number incorrectly.

Knowing what to round each number off to needs some thought. It is no good rounding off to numbers that you cannot mentally check.

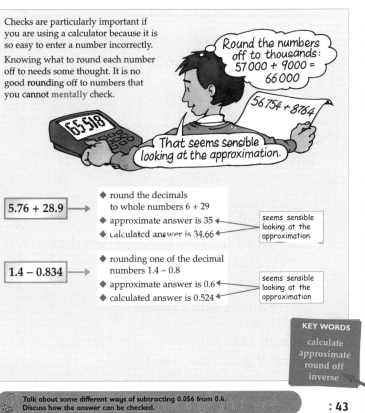

Round the numbers off to thousands:
57 000 + 9 000 = 66 000

56 754 + 8764

That seems sensible looking at the approximation.

5.76 + 28.9
- round the decimals to whole numbers 6 + 29
- approximate answer is 35
- calculated answer is 34.66

seems sensible looking at the approximation

1.4 – 0.834
- rounding one of the decimal numbers 1.4 – 0.8
- approximate answer is 0.6
- calculated answer is 0.524

seems sensible looking at the approximation

KEY WORDS

calculate
approximate
round off
inverse

Talk about some different ways of subtracting 0.056 from 0.4.
Discuss how the answer can be checked.

: 43

The key words are ones that you need to know and use correctly when you write about this topic in mathematics. Make sure you can spell each one and know what it means.

The activities will help you to find out if you have understood the ideas and have mastered the skill. You may need to do some of them in the classroom, but many can be done at home.

MULTIPLY AND DIVIDE BY 10, 100 AND 1000

When you multiply or divide a number by 10, 100 and 1000 the position of each digit in the number moves.

- When you multiply by 10, 100 or 1000 the digits move to the left.
- When you divide by 10, 100 or 1000 the digits move to the right.

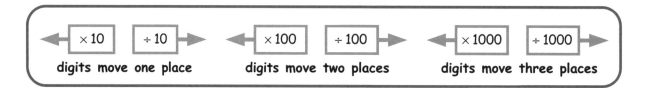

$\times 10$	$\div 10$		$\times 100$	$\div 100$		$\times 1000$	$\div 1000$
digits move one place			digits move two places			digits move three places	

Multiply by 10, 100 and 1000
← digits move to the **left**
$$75$$
$$75 \times 10 = 750$$
$$75 \times 100 = 7500$$
$$75 \times 1000 = 75\,000$$

Divide by 10, 100 and 1000
digits move to the **right** →
$$45\,000$$
$$45\,000 \div 10 = 4500$$
$$45\,000 \div 100 = 450$$
$$45\,000 \div 1000 = 45$$

Adding and taking off zeros

Whole numbers

Zeros added to the end change the value of the number.

$75 \rightarrow 750 \rightarrow 7500 \rightarrow 75\,000$
$\rightarrow$ getting larger

Zeros taken off the end change the value of the number.

$75\,000 \rightarrow 7500 \rightarrow 750 \rightarrow 75$
$\rightarrow$ getting smaller

Decimal numbers

Zeros added to the end **do not** change the value of the number.

$7.5 \rightarrow 7.50 \rightarrow 7.500 \rightarrow 7.5000$
$\rightarrow$ all the same value

Zeros placed between the decimal and digit change the value.

$0.5 \rightarrow 0.05 \rightarrow 0.005 \rightarrow 0.0005$
$\rightarrow$ getting smaller

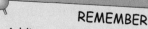

REMEMBER
Adding noughts when multiplying by 10, 100 or 1000 only works with whole numbers. It does not work with decimals.

Use a calculator. Keep multiplying a decimal number by 10. What happens to the digits? Divide a decimal number by 10. What happens to the digits?

Money and measurements

Think carefully how many places a digit will move when money or measurements are multiplied and divided by 10, 100 and 1000. Check first – should the answer be larger or smaller than what you started with?

How many £100 notes are in £85 000?

How many 10p coins total £150?

What is one tenth of £2.50?

What is one hundredth of 3.5 metres?

Metric units of measurements increase and decrease by 10, 100 or 1000.

10 dm = 1 m	100 cm = 1 m	1000 mm = 1 m	1000 m = 1 km
10 dl = 1 l	100 cl = 1 l	1000 ml = 1 l	
1000 g = 1 kg	1000 kg = 1 tonne		

Look very carefully at the units you have to work in.

1 cm × 1000 = ? m
1 km ÷ 1000 = ? cm

100 ml × 100 = ? litres
1 litre ÷ 10 = ? cl

100 g × 100 = ? kg
1 kg ÷ 10 = ? g

KEY WORDS

place value
digits
powers of 10
increasing
decreasing

Find out about prefixes on measuring words. They show whether units are 10, 100 or 1000 times larger than a smaller unit or are $\frac{1}{10}$ $\frac{1}{100}$ $\frac{1}{1000}$ of a larger unit.

ROUNDING AND APPROXIMATING NUMBERS

When you round numbers the half-way position is important.

Round up **numbers that are** half-way or more.

Round down **numbers that are** less than half-way.

- We round numbers to remember them more easily.
- We round numbers when an exact answer is not needed and an approximate one will do.
- You have to decide whether to round numbers to the nearest 10, 100 or 1000.

Rounding to the nearest 10

up to 684 ⇒ round down
685 and above ⇒ round up

*when the **units** digit is 5 or more you round up*

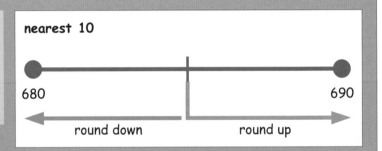

Rounding to the nearest 100

up to 349 ⇒ round down
350 and above ⇒ round up

*when the **tens** digit is 5 or more you round up*

Rounding to the nearest 1000

up to 8499 ⇒ round down
8500 and above ⇒ round up

*when the **hundreds** digit is 5 or more you round up*

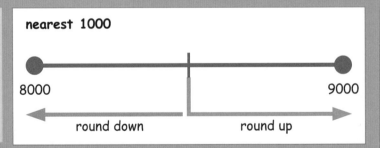

Sometimes when you round up there is a knock on into other columns:

Round 24 996 to the nearest 10 ⇒ 25 000
Round 9960 to the nearest 100 ⇒ 10 000
Round 149 985 to the nearest 1000 ⇒ 150 000

 Use a calculator and work out approximately how many days you have been alive.

Using approximation skills

Rounding can help you find approximate answers to your calculations.

3896 + 6239 round ⇒ 4000 + 6000
The approximate answer is 10 000.
The exact answer is 10 135.

296 × 53 round each number ⇒ 300 × 50
The approximate answer is 15 000.
The exact answer is 15 688.

You will need to decide whether to round to the nearest 10, 100 or 1000 when answering problems.

Approximation is particularly important when measuring. You will often need to measure to the nearest centimetre or metre. It is quite difficult to measure exactly.

REMEMBER
When you round quite large numbers the approximation becomes less accurate.

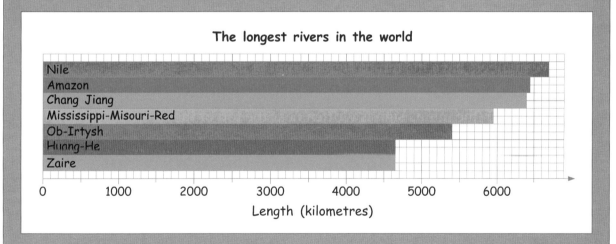

The longest rivers in the world

Nile
Amazon
Chang Jiang
Mississippi-Misouri-Red
Ob-Irtysh
Huang-He
Zaire

0   1000   2000   3000   4000   5000   6000
Length (kilometres)

◆ Are the distances shown on the graph exact or approximate?
◆ Do you think that the Huang-He and Zaire are exactly the same length?
◆ Some reference books give slightly different facts about these river lengths. Why do you think this is so?

KEY WORDS
approximate
approximately
approximation
round up
round down
round off
nearly
about
close
there abouts

8 km is approximately 5 miles. What is the approximate length of each river in miles? Use a calculator to help you.

NUMBERS ON A NUMBER LINE

Number lines show numbers in order.

The position of zero on a number line is important because it separates negative numbers from positive numbers. In between the whole numbers are fractions.

- Integers are whole numbers and zero.
- Integers can be negative or positive.
- Negative numbers can be fractions.

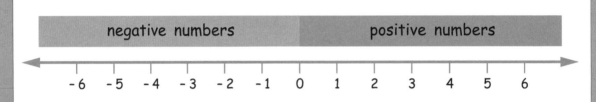

From zero moving to the left the numbers are negative and become smaller.

From zero moving to the right the numbers are positive and become larger.

Negative numbers have the minus sign in front of them:

◆ like this −5 (the minus sign is written near the middle of the number),

◆ or like this ⁻5 (the minus sign is written near the top of the number).

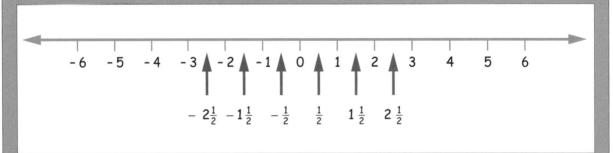

Fractions are numbers between integers.

The fraction can be a mixed number such as $2\frac{1}{2}$.

All the fractions have a place on a number line.

For example all these fractions come between 0 and 1:

$\frac{1}{3}$ $\frac{1}{4}$ $\frac{3}{4}$ $\frac{1}{5}$ $\frac{7}{8}$ $\frac{9}{10}$.

> REMEMBER
> The name for this sign — is minus.

 Name three integers between −2 and 2.

Using positive and negative integers

◆ When you **add** on a number line you move to the **right** ⇒

◆ When you **subtract** on a number line you move to the **left** ⇐

◆ When you subtract a larger number from a smaller one the answer is a negative number.

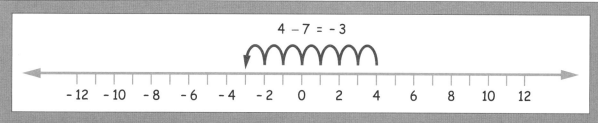

$$4 - 7 = -3$$

−12 −10 −8 −6 −4 −2 0 2 4 6 8 10 12

Cold temperatures use negative numbers.

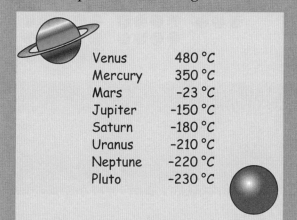

Venus	480 °C
Mercury	350 °C
Mars	-23 °C
Jupiter	-150 °C
Saturn	-180 °C
Uranus	-210 °C
Neptune	-220 °C
Pluto	-230 °C

◆ Venus is warmest and Pluto is coldest.

◆ The temperature difference between Venus and Jupiter is 330 °C. Jupiter is 330° colder than Venus.

◆ The temperature difference between Mars and Neptune is 197 °C. Mars is 197° warmer than Neptune.

KEY WORDS

positive   minus   fraction
negative   plus   integer

Look at this time line.

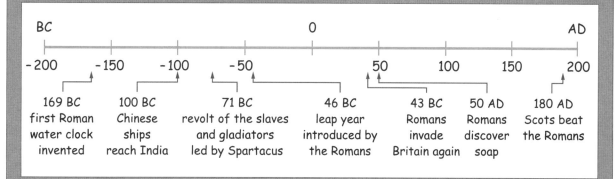

| BC | | | | | 0 | | | | AD |

−200   −150   −100   −50   50   100   150   200

| 169 BC | 100 BC | 71 BC | 46 BC | 43 BC | 50 AD | 180 AD |
| first Roman water clock invented | Chinese ships reach India | revolt of the slaves and gladiators led by Spartacus | leap year introduced by the Romans | Romans invade Britain again | Romans discover soap | Scots beat the Romans |

BC dates are like negative numbers and AD dates like positive numbers.

On a calculator find five subtractions that have an answer of −8.

SPECIAL NUMBERS, PATTERNS AND SEQUENCES

There are some special numbers that you need to recognise. These include odd, even, square and triangular numbers.

The numbers may appear in a sequence or as a repeating pattern of digits.

- Whole numbers are either odd or even numbers.
- Whole numbers can be square numbers or triangular numbers.
- Sequences of numbers often go up or down in similar steps.

Square numbers

These are the result of multiplying a whole number by itself. They can be shown by dots in the form of squares.

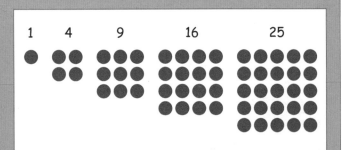

A short way of writing 3×3 is 3^2. We call this the square of 3 or three squared.

To undo a squaring find the square root. The square root of 9 is 3.

A short way of writing square root is $\sqrt{}$.

Triangular numbers

These can be shown by dots in the form of triangles.

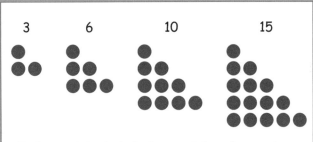

It is usual to include 1 as a triangular number.

If you add next-door triangular numbers you get a square number.

REMEMBER
You can square a number that is not whole but it will not make a square number.

12 Can you discover a triangular number that is also a square number?

Sequences and patterns

Some sequences go up or down in equal-sized steps.

The difference between adjacent numbers will always be the same.

> 24, 26, 28, 30, ... ⟹ even numbers
>
> 301, 299, 297, 295, ... ⟹ odd numbers

Sequences can be integers, fractions or decimals.

> −11, −7, −3, 1 ⟹ step is +4
>
> $\frac{1}{4}, \frac{1}{2}, \frac{3}{4}, 1$ ⟹ step is +$\frac{1}{4}$
>
> 2.0, 2.25, 2.5, 2.75, 3.0 ⟹ step is + 0.25

Some sequences go up or down in different sized steps.

> A sequence of square numbers:
> 81, 100, 121, 144 ⟹
>
> A sequence of triangular numbers:
> 10, 15, 21, 28 ⟹

Halving and doubling makes sequences with different sized steps.

> A halving sequence: 2, 1, $\frac{1}{2}$, $\frac{1}{4}$ ⟹
>
> A doubling sequence: 0.1, 0.2, 0.4, 0.8 ⟹

REMEMBER
If you have to find missing numbers in sequences always check whether it goes up or down in equal-sized steps.

Sometimes you have to recognise special numbers that are in a line but not in a sequence.

> Which are
> odd numbers? 347, 703, 274, 518, 649
>
> Which are
> square numbers? 45, 81, 35, 25, 56

Digits in numbers can also make repeating patterns.

> 9.09090909
> 4.545454545

KEY WORDS
square number
triangular number
sequence
step
pattern

 Try to find a calculator division that makes a repeating pattern of digits.

MULTIPLES AND MULTIPLYING

You should be able to instantly recognise multiples up to 10×10.

You can use the multiples you know to quickly work out multiples you don't know.

- Multiples do not stop at the tenth multiple.
- Some numbers are common multiples.
- Some multiples can be recognised instantly.

A multiple is lots of the same number or quantity like the multiplication tables.

Multiples of 7 are: 7, 14, 21, 28, 35

They carry on and on. Multiples of 7 include numbers such as 77, 700 and 1400. Any number that can be divided exactly by 7 is a multiple of 7.

Multiples that are easy to spot

Multiples of 9 have digits that total 9 or a multiple of 9 → 45, 81, 99, 144	Multiples of 3 have digits that total 3 or a multiple of 3 → 27, 45, 66, 132
Multiples of 6 are even and are divisible by 3 → 24, 42, 66, 132	Multiples of 25 end in 25, 50, 75 or 00 → 125, 175, 650, 900

The order of multiplying

The order in which you multiply does not matter.

◆ The fifth multiple of six equals the sixth multiple of five.

◆ The answer of 30 is a multiple of both 5 and 6.

If you know the 5th multiple of 6 you can work out multiples such as the 50th and 500th:

$6 \times 5 = 30$ so $6 \times 50 = 300$ and $6 \times 500 = 3000$.

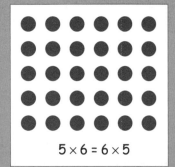

$5 \times 6 = 6 \times 5$

REMEMBER
Not all sequences that go up by the same number are multiples.

 Half of some numbers are all divisible by 4.
Which multiples could the numbers be?

Common multiples

To find the smallest common multiple of a pair of numbers start off with the larger number and say each multiple in turn. When you come to a multiple that is divisible by the smaller number then that is the smallest common multiple.

Numbers can be multiples of more than one number.

◆ **12** is a common multiple of 2, 3, 4, and 6.
◆ Some common multiples of 3 and 4 are **12, 24, 36, 48**.
◆ All these numbers are divisible by both 3 and 4.
◆ The smallest common multiple of 3 and 4 is **12**.

Multiples of …	are also multiples of …
4, 6, 8, 10, … ⟶	**2**
6, 9, 12, 15, … ⟶	**3**
8, 12, 16, 20, … ⟶	**4**

> **HINT**
> To find the smallest common multiple of three numbers start off with the larger number and say each multiple in turn. When you come to a multiple that is divisible by both the other two numbers then that is the smallest common multiple.

Finding multiples of large numbers

To find some multiples of 12 you can:

◆ double any multiple of 6,
◆ triple any multiple of 4.

To find some multiples of 18 you can:

◆ double any multiple of 9,
◆ triple any multiple of 6.

KEY WORDS

multiple
common multiple
divisible

Can you find a rule for which numbers produce odd multiples?

FACTORS

Factors of a number will divide exactly into that number. A number is exactly divisible by its factors.

The prime factors of a number are particularly important.

- Factors of a number can be written in order.
- Factors of a number can be written in pairs.
- Some factors of a number are prime numbers.

The factors of a number can be written in order

The factors of 12 in order are: 1, 2, 3, 4, 6, 12

The factors of 18 in order are: 1, 2, 3, 6, 9, 18

The factors of 36 in order are: 1, 2, 3, 4, 6, 9, 12, 18, 36

Apart from the number itself, notice that no factor is greater than half of the number.

Notice that 1 and the number itself are both factors of a number.

The factors of a number can be written in matching pairs

The factors of 12 in pairs are: (1,12) (2,6) (3,4)

The factors of 18 in pairs are: (1,18) (2,9) (3,6)

The factors of 36 in pairs are: (1,36) (2,18) (3,12) (4,9) (6,6)

Usually the smaller of the pair is written first.

The factors of 100 are particularly important.

(1,100) (2,50) (4,25) (5,20) (10,10)

There are not as many as you might think.

REMEMBER
A smaller number can have many more factors than a larger number.

Find out which sort of numbers have an odd number of factors when placed in order.

Prime factors

Prime numbers have only two factors, themselves and one.

The only even prime number is 2.

A common mistake is to think that 1 is a prime number.

The smallest prime number is 2.

1 is odd, square and triangular but it is not prime.

It is not prime because it has only one factor and not two.

3 5 17
2 11
19 23 13

You will need to recognise the prime factors of a number.

The factors of 12 in order are: 1, 2, 3, 4, 6, and 12.
Its prime factors are 2 and 3.

The factors of 15 in order are: 1, 3, 5, and 15.
Its prime factors are 3 and 5.

The factors of 22 in order are: 1, 2, 11 and 22.
Its prime factors are 2 and 11.

Eratosthenes was a Greek mathematician who lived 275–195 BC. His number sieve was a way to find all the prime numbers less than 100.

Cross out 1
Leave 2 but cross out all multiples of 2
Leave 3 but cross out all multiples of 3
Leave 5 but cross out all multiples of 5
Leave 7 but cross out all multiples of 7

The numbers not crossed out are all prime numbers.

KEY WORDS

divisor
factor
divisible
prime number
prime factor

1	2	3	4	5	6	7	8	9	10
11	12	13	14	15	16	17	18	19	20
21	22	23	24	25	26	27	28	29	30
31	32	33	34	35	36	37	38	39	40
41	42	43	44	45	46	47	48	49	50
51	52	53	54	55	56	57	58	59	60
61	62	63	64	65	66	67	68	69	70
71	72	73	74	75	76	77	78	79	80
81	82	83	84	85	86	87	88	89	90
91	92	93	94	95	96	97	98	99	100

 TRUE or FALSE? There is always a prime number between consecutive square numbers up to 100.

VULGAR AND IMPROPER FRACTIONS

A vulgar fraction is another name for a common, proper or simple fraction. It has a larger denominator than numerator.

Improper fractions are top heavy, they have a larger numerator than denominator.

A mixed number consists of a whole number and a proper fraction.

- ● Vulgar fractions have their numerator less than their denominator.
- ● Improper fractions have their numerator greater than their denominator.
- ● Improper fractions can be changed into a mixed numbers.

Vulgar fractions

A vulgar fraction lies between 0 and 1 on a number line. It is less than 1.

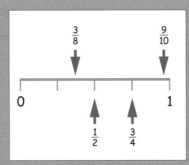

$\frac{2} \leftarrow$ numerator
$\frac{}{3} \leftarrow$ denominator

The numerator is smaller than the denominator.

vulgar comes from the Latin word *vulgaris* meaning common

fraction comes from a Latin word *fractum* meaning to break

Improper fractions

An improper fraction has a larger numerator than denominator. It is worth more than 1.

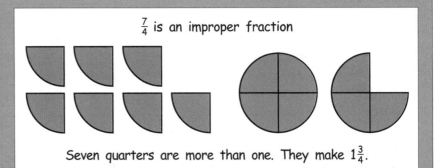

$\frac{7}{4}$ is an improper fraction

Seven quarters are more than one. They make $1\frac{3}{4}$.

Mixed numbers

A mixed number has whole numbers and fractions.

These are all mixed numbers: $1\frac{2}{3}$ $2\frac{1}{2}$ $7\frac{3}{4}$ $12\frac{9}{10}$ $15\frac{4}{5}$

You can have negative mixed numbers such as $-2\frac{1}{2}$.

REMEMBER
Mixed numbers are not integers.

 Write five improper fractions that lie between 2 and 3 on a number line.

Changing mixed numbers

You can change improper fractions into mixed numbers.

$$\frac{7}{4} = 1\frac{3}{4}$$

seven quarters makes one whole one with three quarters left over

$$\frac{11}{3} = 3\frac{2}{3}$$

eleven thirds makes three whole ones with two thirds left over

Sometimes you need to change a mixed number into an improper fraction.

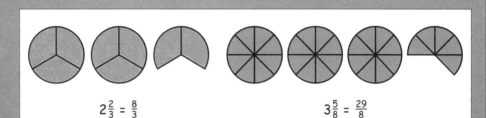

$$2\frac{2}{3} = \frac{8}{3}$$

$$3\frac{5}{8} = \frac{29}{8}$$

There is a link between fractions and division.

$15 \div 4$ is the same as $\frac{15}{4}$

Writing a division as an improper fraction lets you work out the quotient as a mixed number.

The quotient of $15 \div 4$ is $\frac{15}{4}$ which equals $3\frac{3}{4}$.

About quotients

A quotient is the number resulting from a division.

$15 \div 4 = 3$ remainder 3

The quotient is 3 with a remainder of 3.

$15 \div 4 = 3\frac{3}{4}$

The quotient is $3\frac{3}{4}$.

KEY WORDS

vulgar fraction
improper fraction
mixed number
numerator
denominator
integer
quotient

Write five mixed numbers that lie between $4\frac{1}{2}$ and $5\frac{1}{2}$.

EQUIVALENCE

When two or more things are equivalent they look different but are worth the same.

Cancelling a fraction makes an equivalent fraction with a smaller numerator and denominator.

- Equivalent fractions look different but are worth the same.
- You cancel a fraction by dividing top and bottom by the same number.
- You simplify a fraction by cancelling.

You use equivalence in most areas of mathematics not just fractions. Equivalence is all about swapping things worth the same. It is also about making the best swap possible to answer the problem.

Equivalent fractions

$$\frac{1}{2} = \frac{2}{4} = \frac{3}{6} = \frac{4}{8} = \frac{5}{10}$$

The denominators in each set are multiples of the same number.

The numerators in each set are also multiples of the same number.

$$\frac{2}{3} = \frac{4}{6} = \frac{6}{9} = \frac{8}{12} = \frac{10}{15}$$

You can change thirds into sixths, ninths, twelfths and fifteenths but not into eighths or tenths. This is because eight and ten are not multiples of three.

Making equivalent fractions

Multiply the top and bottom of the fraction by the same number.

To change $\frac{2}{3}$ to twelfths multiply top and bottom by 4.

$$\frac{2^{\times 4}}{3_{\times 4}} = \frac{8}{12}$$

REMEMBER
The denominator decides which equivalent fractions you can make.

 Explain why fifths cannot be changed into eighths.

Cancelling fractions

Cancelling is about using equivalence to make a fraction simpler. To simplify a fraction you make the denominator as small as possible. The simplified fraction must still be equivalent to the fraction you started with.

To simplify a fraction divide the top and bottom of the fraction by the same number.

To simplify $\frac{8}{12}$ divide top and bottom by 4.

$$\frac{8 \div 4}{12 \div 4} = \frac{2}{3}$$

The difficult part is deciding which number will divide exactly into the top and bottom. It is no good choosing a number that will only divide into one of them.

Sometimes you can cancel more than once.

$$\frac{20 \div 2}{24 \div 2} = \frac{10}{12} \qquad \frac{10 \div 2}{12 \div 2} = \frac{5}{6}$$

It would have been slightly quicker to divide by 4 in the first place.

KEY WORDS

multiple
numerator
denominator
equivalent fraction
cancel
simplify

All that really matters is that you cancel down until the denominator is as small as possible.

Hundredths are important because we use them in fractions, decimals and percentages. It is helpful to remember what they can be cancelled down to.

Hundredths can be changed to: halves, quarters, fifths, tenths, twentieths, twenty-fifths and fiftieths.

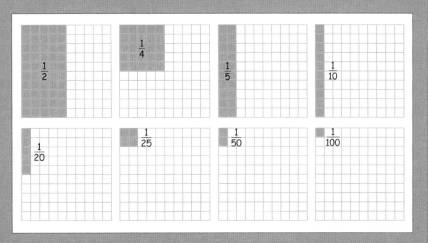

What is the difference between a simple fraction and a simplified fraction?

21

DENOMINATORS

When you have to order and compare fractions it is helpful to use equivalent fractions that have the same denominator. This is called finding the common denominator.

- When comparing fractions change them to a common denominator.
- You can find the fraction of a fraction.

Comparing fractions

It is easy to order or compare fractions when the denominators are the same.

$$\frac{3}{8} < \frac{7}{8} \qquad \frac{5}{8} > \frac{3}{8}$$

comparing fractions

$$\frac{1}{8}, \frac{3}{8}, \frac{4}{8}, \frac{6}{8}$$

ordering fractions

It is not so easy to compare and order when the denominators are different.

Which is larger $\frac{2}{3}$ or $\frac{3}{4}$?

Change the denominators to the same number to make it easier.

$$\frac{8}{12} \qquad \frac{9}{12}$$

Thirds and quarters can be changed to twelfths.

So two thirds is less than three quarters.

$$\frac{2}{3} < \frac{3}{4}$$

REMEMBER
< means is less than
> means is greater than
The arrow head always points to the smaller number.

When both fractions have the same denominator we say they have a common denominator.

You have to choose the common denominator for the fractions you are comparing.

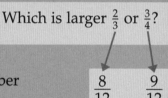

Suggest a fraction that is greater than a quarter but less than a third.
Think about changing both fractions to twelfths.

Comparing fractions and half way points

It is useful to be able to compare fractions to see how much larger or smaller one is than the other.

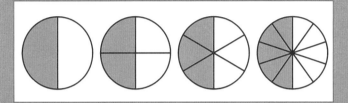

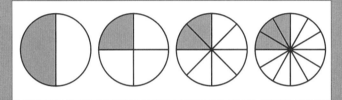

A half is twice as much as a quarter.

A half is three times as much as a sixth.

A half is five times as much as a tenth.

A quarter is half as much as a half.

A quarter is twice as much as an eighth.

A quarter is three times as much as a twelfth.

Half way points

We sometimes need to work out the half way positions between numbers and fractions.

Which fraction is half way between $\frac{1}{4}$ and $\frac{1}{2}$?

If you put in all the half way marks you get eighths.

You can now see that half way between $\frac{1}{4}$ and $\frac{1}{2}$ is $\frac{3}{8}$.

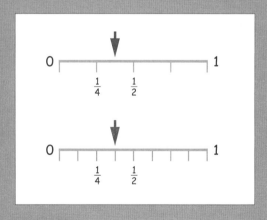

KEY WORDS

common denominator
equivalent fractions
compare
greater than
less than

Which of these denominators will produce most equivalent fractions: 15, 24 or 30?

FRACTIONS OF QUANTITIES

You can find fractional amounts of numbers and measurements.

The denominator tells you how many equal parts there are. The numerator lets you know the number of those equal parts that are required.

> ● To find a fraction of a quantity divide by the denominator and multiply by the numerator.
>
> ● When finding one measurement as a fraction of another the units must be the same.

When the numerator is 1

$\frac{1}{5}$ of 125 $\Rightarrow$ a fifth of 125 is 125 ÷ 5 $\Rightarrow$ answer 25

the denominator tells you that 5 equal parts are needed

When the numerator is more than 1

the numerator tells you that 3 of the equal parts are needed

$\frac{3}{5}$ of 125 $\Rightarrow$ one fifth of 125 is 25
three fifths of 125 is 3 × 25 $\Rightarrow$ answer 75

the denominator tells you that 5 equal parts are needed

It is important to be able to find tenths and hundredths of numbers.

$\frac{3}{10}$ of 75 $\Rightarrow$ one tenth of 75 is 7.5 $\Rightarrow$ three tenths of 75 is 22.5

$\frac{30}{100}$ of 80 $\Rightarrow$ one hundredth of 80 is 0.8 $\Rightarrow$ thirty hundredths of 80 is 24

◆ Notice how the answer need not always be a whole number.

◆ Sometimes you will be able to change the hundredths into tenths. This could be quicker.

REMEMBER
Answers can be a whole number, fraction, mixed number or decimal.

Find some simple fractions of 100 that will not produce an answer that is a whole number.

Fractions and measurements

You will need to find fractions of measurements. You may also have to work out what one measurement is as a fraction of another.

A very important decision will have to be made:

which unit of measurement shall I work in?

Your choice can make the problem easier or more difficult than necessary.

Look carefully at the unit of measurement and decide whether to work in that unit or change it to smaller units.

$\frac{3}{8}$ of 1 kg $\Rightarrow$ one eighth of 1000 g is 125 g
three eighths of 1000 g is 375 g

Remember you may not need to change the unit.

Choosing suitable units is very important when finding one measurement as a fraction of another.

You might have to choose whether to cancel a fraction.

Sometimes it is more useful not to cancel a fraction.

For example $\frac{35}{100}$ may be easier to work with than cancelling it to $\frac{7}{20}$.

What fraction of £1 is 35p?	Working in pennies the fraction is $\frac{35}{100}$.
What fraction of a kilogram is 375 g?	Working in grams the fraction is $\frac{375}{1000}$.
What fraction of a year is 1 week?	Working in weeks the fraction is $\frac{1}{52}$.

You can often change hundredths into other fractions.
Think about when it is easier to leave the fraction in hundredths.

RATIO AND PROPORTION

Ratio is used to compare two or more quantities. A ratio of 1 to 2 means something is twice as much as something else.

Scales on maps use ratio. A scale of 1 : 25 000 means each cm on the map stands for 25 000 cm on the ground.

- In ratios you need to work out how many parts there are altogether.
- Scale drawings, models and maps all use ratio and proportion.
- If you change things in proportion all the measurements alter in the same ratio.

Problem: *Build a rod with red and yellow cubes. For each two red cubes use three yellow cubes. How long can the rods be?*

Think about how many cubes the smallest model must have.

Because there are two red to every three yellow the rod must have 5 cubes.

The next sizes must have 10, 15, 20, ... cubes.

As the rod gets longer the ratio of two red to three yellow remains.

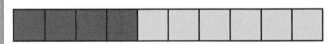

the ratio of red to yellow is 2 to 3

the longer rod still has two reds to every three yellow

Problem: *What fraction of each rod is red when two red cubes are used for each three yellow cubes?*

For each two red cubes there are three yellow cubes. In the whole rod there must be 5 or a multiple of 5 cubes.

The fractions must be in fifths.

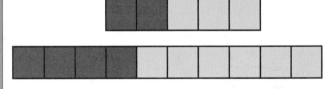

$\frac{2}{5}$ of each of the rod is red $\frac{3}{5}$ is yellow

> **REMEMBER**
>
> In ratios many people get the fraction wrong. If there is 1 white cube to each 3 black cubes then $\frac{1}{4}$ is white NOT $\frac{1}{3}$.
>
> This is because you must use at least 4 cubes or a multiple of 4.

 A rod has 24 cubes, some black and some white. What could the ratios of black to white be?

Scale and proportion

A scale of 1 : 200 means the plan is $\frac{1}{200}$ of the real thing. Each 1 cm on the plan equals 200 cm in the real house.

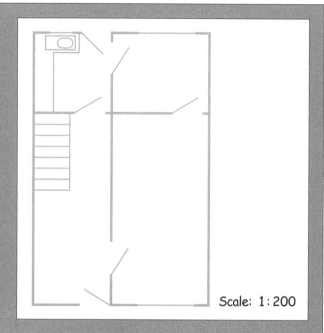

Scale: 1 : 200

When you keep things in proportion all the measurements must change by the same fraction or ratio.

This has changed in proportion. All the measurements have changed in the same ratio.

This has not changed in proportion. The height has changed in a different proportion to the width.

KEY WORDS

ratio
proportion
per
in every
for every

 Explain what travelling at 50 km per hour means.

DECIMALS

Decimals are based on ten. A decimal fraction is a type of fraction where a number of tenths, hundredths and thousandths are shown by the digits to the right of the decimal point. The decimal point lies between digits worth units or ones and digits worth $\frac{1}{10}$.

Metric measurements are based on decimals.

- Digits to the left of the decimal point increase by 10, 100, 1000 →
- Digits to the right of the decimal point decrease by $\frac{1}{10}$, $\frac{1}{100}$, $\frac{1}{1000}$ →
- The decimal point separates whole units from fractions of a unit.

Each digit in a decimal has a value.

2 whole units   3 units 4 hundredths   2 tens 1 tenth 5 thousandths

2.7   **3.94**   **26.125**

7 tenths   9 tenths   6 units   2 hundredths

You can write and say the fraction part of a decimal in different ways.

When you look at each digit in turn it says six tenths, two hundredths and five thousandths.

$$0.625 \longrightarrow \frac{625}{1000} = \frac{6}{10} + \frac{2}{100} + \frac{5}{1000}$$

When you look at the complete decimal fraction it says six hundred and twenty-five thousandths.

The value of a digit changes depending on its position in relation to the decimal point.

REMEMBER
The position of the zeros in decimal numbers is important.
0.5 = 0.50 = 0.5000 these are equal
0.5 ≠ 0.05 ≠ 0.005 these are not equal

Talk about the decimal numbers you can make with the digits 2 and 5. You can use as many zeros as you want.

Using decimals

You will find decimals used in measurements and money. The decimal point in measurements separates the whole units from the fractions of a unit.

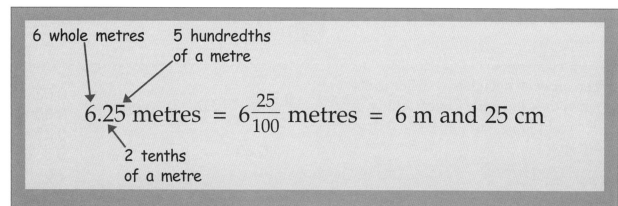

6 whole metres   5 hundredths of a metre

$$6.25 \text{ metres} = 6\frac{25}{100} \text{ metres} = 6 \text{ m and } 25 \text{ cm}$$

2 tenths of a metre

Decimal measurements can be written in different ways.

the 6.25 m has been multiplied by 100 to change it to centimetres (there are 100 cm in 1 metre)

$$6.25 \text{ m} = 625 \text{ cm} = 6250 \text{ mm}$$

the 6.25 m has been multiplied by 1000 to change it to millimetres (there are 1000 mm in 1 metre)

When reading scales it is important to work out what each mark is worth. They can be worth numbers such as 2, 5, 10, 20, 50, 100, 200 or 1000.

Here is part of a long metre tape. The longer marks are tenths of a metre and the shorter ones are hundredths of a metre.

0.5 m is 50 cm or 500 mm

KEY WORDS

place value
digits
decimal point
decimal places
decimal fraction

Enter a digit on a calculator and explore multiplying and dividing by powers of 10. What happens to the decimal point?

POSITIONING AND ORDERING DECIMALS

It is easier to work with decimals when they have the same number of decimal places. Careful use of zeros can make decimals have the same number of places.

- Line up the decimal points when ordering decimals.
- Ordering is usually smallest to largest.
- The units should be the same when ordering.

The order of decimals is easier to see when they have the same number of decimal places and the decimal points are aligned.

0.3	3.0	0.05
0.25	0.03	

0.03
0.05
0.25
0.3
3.0

Zeros placed after the other digits do not alter the value in a decimal number.

$$0.2 = 0.20 = 0.200 = 0.2000$$

Using number lines

Not all the numbers are labelled on a number line.
You have to quickly work out the position of some numbers.

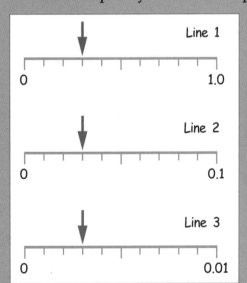

- ◆ Look at the numbers given on each line.
- ◆ Note that the marks are in tenths.
- ◆ Work out the value of each mark.
- ◆ Line 1 has marks worth 0.1.
- ◆ Line 2 has marks worth 0.01.
- ◆ Line 3 has marks worth 0.001.

REMEMBER
A common mistake is to think that smaller numbers have most decimal places. 0.634533 is not smaller than 0.2 but is smaller than 0.7. You need to look carefully at the digit after the decimal point for clues.

Write as many numbers as you can using a decimal point and the digits 3, 5 and 7. Put the numbers in order.

Ordering measurements

You might have to order numbers that are a mix of decimals, whole numbers and fractions. When ordering mixed numbers it helps if they are the 'same sort' of number.

Problem: *What is the order of these lengths starting with the smallest?*

2.05 m $2\frac{3}{4}$ m 260 cm 2.5 m

Decimals are easier to compare and order.

The measurement units should all be the same.

2.05 m 2.75 m 2.60 m 2.50 m
(or 205 cm 275 cm 260 cm 250 cm)

Then put them in the right order.

2.05 m 2.50 m 2.60 m 2.75 m

You might have to change the units back to the original.

2.05 m 2.5 m 260 cm $2\frac{3}{4}$ m

KEY WORDS

> greater than, more than, larger than
< less than, smaller than, fewer than
= equal, equivalent, same value

Explain how these measurements could be entered into a calculator:
$3\frac{3}{4}$ kg, $1\frac{3}{10}$ m, $4\frac{1}{2}$ km.

ROUNDING DECIMALS

Rounding decimals gives a sensible approximation with which to work. You often round decimals to the nearest whole number or the nearest tenth.

Another way of saying round to the nearest tenth is round to one decimal place.

⦿ To round to the nearest whole number look at the tenths digit. If it is 5 or more you round up to the next whole number.

⦿ To round to the nearest tenth look at the hundredths digit. If it is 5 or more you round up to the next tenth.

When rounding decimals to the nearest whole number you have to decide whether to round up or round down. The value of the tenths digit tells you which. Half way (0.5) or more rounds up.

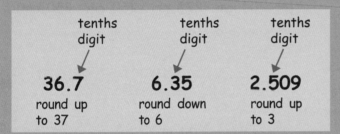

tenths digit	tenths digit	tenths digit
36.7	**6.35**	**2.509**
round up to 37	round down to 6	round up to 3

◆ The tenths digit is the first one after the decimal point.

◆ If the tenths digit is 5 or more you round up to the next whole number.

When rounding decimals to the nearest tenth or to one decimal place you have to decide whether to round up or round down. The value of the hundredth digit tells you which. Half way (0.05) or more rounds up.

hundredths digit	hundredths digit	hundredths digit
0.57	**1.348**	**0.555**
round up to 0.6	round down to 1.3	round up to 0.6

◆ The hundredths digit is the second one after the decimal point.

◆ If the hundredths digit is 5 or more you round up to the next tenth.

> **REMEMBER**
> When you round a number there can be a knock on effect to other digits.
> 3.99 rounded to the nearest tenth is 4.0.

 Try to work out a rule for rounding to the nearest hundredth or two places of decimals.

Rounding measurements

You will sometimes need to round measurements off to the nearest whole unit or tenth. The same rules apply as if they were numbers not measurements.

Rounding to the nearest whole unit

- Half way or more between whole units you round up.
- The tenth digit shows which is half way or more.

Rounding to the nearest tenth, or one decimal place

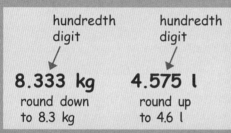

- Measuring to the nearest tenth in kilograms is the same as to the nearest 100 g.
- Measuring to the nearest tenth in litres is the same as to the nearest 100 ml.

Sometimes rounding to the nearest 10 or 100 is accurate enough. At other times you need to be slightly more accurate.

The distance between two cities is 473.55 km.

473.55 km ≈ 474 km (nearest km)
473.55 km ≈ 475 km (nearest 5 km)
473.55 km ≈ 470 km (nearest 10 km)

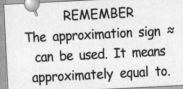

REMEMBER
The approximation sign ≈ can be used. It means approximately equal to.

Should you round to the nearest km, nearest 5 km or nearest 10 km?

It depends on what the measurement is going to be used for and how accurate you need to be.

KEY WORDS

roughly   round up
exactly   round down
approximate   round off
approximation

Talk about why we do not often measure to the nearest gram or nearest millilitre. It is more likely to be to the nearest 10 g or 10 ml, or even nearest 100 g or 100 ml.

33

FRACTIONS AND DECIMALS

Both fractions and decimals deal with parts of numbers or quantities.

You can change vulgar fractions into decimal fractions if that makes the problem simpler.

You need to know the equivalent decimals for simple fractions.

- Some fractions change into decimals exactly but some do not.
- You can change a fraction into a decimal by dividing the denominator into the numerator.
- Decimals are usually easier to work with than fractions.

You should remember these common fractions as decimals.

$\frac{1}{2} = 0.5$	$\frac{1}{4} = 0.25$	$\frac{3}{4} = 0.75$	$\frac{1}{5} = 0.2$
$\frac{1}{10} = 0.1$	$\frac{1}{100} = 0.01$	$\frac{1}{1000} = 0.001$	

Thirds do not change into a decimal exactly. The decimal equivalent is a recurring decimal that goes on and on and on ...

$\frac{1}{3} = 0.3333333333 ...$	$\frac{2}{3} = 0.66666666667...$
This is usually rounded to 0.333.	This is usually rounded to 0.667.

You can change any fraction into a decimal by dividing the denominator into the numerator.

$$\frac{5}{8} = 8\overline{)5.000} = 0.625$$

Some fractions do not change into a decimal exactly. You have to approximate these to two or three decimal places.

$$\frac{3}{7} = 7\overline{)3.0000} = 0.4285714 ...$$
$$\frac{3}{7} \approx 0.429$$

REMEMBER
If you know the unit fraction as a decimal you can work out others by multiplying:
$\frac{1}{8}$ = 0.125 so $\frac{3}{8}$ = 3 × 0.125 and $\frac{5}{8}$ = 5 × 0.125

 Which member of the sixth family will change to an exact decimal?

Parts of measurements

You can work in fractions of measurements or decimals. It is useful to be able to change from decimals to fractions and from fractions to decimals.

A decimal measurement can be written in different ways, all of which are equivalent.

8.75 m = 8 m and 75 cm = 875 cm = $8\frac{3}{4}$ m

4.125 kg = 4 kg and 125 g = 4125 g = $4\frac{1}{8}$ kg

2.35 m is equivalent to $2\frac{35}{100}$ m $\Rightarrow$ a hundredth of a metre is 1 cm
so 2.35 m = 235 cm

4.305 kg is equivalent to $4\frac{305}{1000}$ kg $\Rightarrow$ a thousandth of a kilogram is 1 g so 4.305 = 4305 g

2125 ml is equivalent to $2\frac{125}{1000}$ l $\Rightarrow$ a thousandth of a litre is 1 ml
so 2.125 l = 2125 ml

$\frac{125}{100}$ can be simplified to $\frac{1}{8}$ $\Rightarrow$ so 2.125 l also = $2\frac{1}{8}$ l

These are all equivalent.

KEY WORDS

recurring decimal
decimal place
equivalent
approximately
vulgar fraction
decimal fraction

Write these fractions in order: $\frac{9}{20}, \frac{7}{15}, \frac{13}{40}, \frac{11}{25}$. It will help to change them into decimals first.

PERCENTAGES

A percentage shows a fraction out of 100.

The percentage sign % looks a bit like a cross between 100 and a fraction.

Fractions must be changed to hundredths before they can be written as a percentage.

- A percentage is another way of showing hundredths.
- The sign for percentage is %.
- A percentage can be written as a fraction.
- Hundredths can be written as a fraction or as a decimal.

Changing percentages to fractions

Percentages are easily changed to hundredths. You may be able to simplify after this.

$40\% = \frac{40}{100}$	$5\% = \frac{5}{100}$
$65\% = \frac{65}{100}$	$99\% = \frac{99}{100}$

Changing fractions to percentages

Fractions must be out of 100 before they can be written as percentages.

$\frac{1}{2} = \frac{50}{100} = 50\%$	$\frac{3}{4} = \frac{75}{100} = 75\%$
$\frac{1}{10} = \frac{10}{100} = 10\%$	$\frac{1}{5} = \frac{20}{100} = 20\%$

A percentage can be written as a fraction or as a decimal.

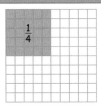

$25\% = 0.25 = \frac{1}{4}$

twenty-five hundreths is one quarter

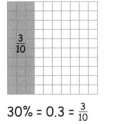

$30\% = 0.3 = \frac{3}{10}$

thirty hundreths is three tenths

Thirds and two-thirds as percentages are interesting.

$\frac{1}{3} = 33\frac{1}{3}\%$ which is approximately 33%

$\frac{2}{3} = 66\frac{2}{3}\%$ which is approximately 67%

REMEMBER
Although percentages are hundredths you can have fractions of a percent such as $2\frac{1}{2}\%$.

 Name three percentages that lie between $\frac{1}{2}$ and $\frac{3}{4}$.

Changing to percentages

You can write one number as a percentage of another after changing to hundredths. The hundredths can be written as fraction or a decimal.

Marks in tests are often changed to percentages: $\frac{67}{100}$ is 67%.

But there are not always 100 marks in a test.

Here are some scores that are changed into percentages.

a score of $\frac{17}{20} = \frac{85}{100} = 85\%$ a score of $\frac{4}{5} = \frac{80}{100} = 80\%$

a score of $\frac{7}{10} = \frac{70}{100} = 70\%$ a score of $\frac{15}{50} = \frac{30}{100} = 30\%$

But what if the total marks scored cannot be changed into hundredths easily?
Remember that hundredths can be decimal fractions as well as vulgar fractions.

Change the fraction to a decimal fraction then write it as a percentage. You might have to round off the decimal to the nearest hundredth.

$7 \times 7 = 4$ ✔
$3 \times 7 = 21$ ✔
$14 + 37 = 52$ ✘
$36 - 7 = 29$ ✔
$5 \times 7 = 35$ ✔
14/30

a score of $\frac{14}{30}$

change to decimal hundredths by dividing 14 by 30

$\frac{14}{30} = 14 \div 30 = 0.47 = 47\%$

Approximately $\frac{2}{3}$ of the globe is covered by water.

$\frac{2}{3} = 2 \div 3 = 0.66666 \ldots = 67\%$

KEY WORDS

percentage
percent
hundredths
proportion

Work out what percentage of your class: are girls, enjoy sport, hate television, wear red.

PERCENTAGES OF NUMBERS AND QUANTITIES

When you find a percentage of something it is helpful to know what 1% and 10% are. Other useful percentages to be able to work out quickly are 50%, 25% and 75%.

- Percentages are hundredths.
- A percentage increase makes something larger.
- A percentage decrease makes something smaller.
- You can use a percentage you know to work out other percentages.

Finding percentages of money should not be too difficult. You can use 1% and 10% to find other percentages. Try to use the facts you know to work out those you don't know.

1% of £1 = 1p	1% of £5 = 5p
10% of £1 = 10p	10% of £5 = 50p
25% of £1 = 25p	25% of £5 = £1.25
50% of £1 = 50p	50% of £5 = £2.50

You will have to understand percentages in measurements. Because percentages are hundredths and metric measures are based on 10, 100 and 1000, this makes things simpler.

10% of 1 kg = 100 g	5% of 1 litre = 50 ml
25% of 1 km = 250 m	1% of 1 m = 1 cm or 10 mm

What is the weight of each ingredient in the recipe?

5% of 500 g =

500g

35% of 500 g =

2% of 500 g =

20% of 500 g =

30% of 500 g =

Eggs and nuts 8% of 500 g =

Recipe
30% dried fruit
5% butter
35% flour
2% sugar
8% eggs and nuts
20% liquid

 Talk about what percentage of the day you spend doing different things.

Percentage gain and loss

Sometimes an amount increases or decreases by a percentage.

First work out how much is taken off for each pound.

> 20% is 20p in £1 or one fifth

Then work out the total amount that is taken off.

> the jeans will have 19 × 20p taken off the price.

Then subtract the amount taken off from the old price to get the new price.

> £15.20

Interest is added to the amount of money. 5% is 5p in £1.

Helen put in £50 and receives interest of 5%.

The interest is 50 × 5p, so £2.50 interest is added to her £50 making £52.50.

> **REMEMBER**
> A common mistake is to work out the percentage then forget to add it on or take it off the starting amount.

VAT is an amount that is added to some things that you buy.

VAT at $17\frac{1}{2}$% is not easy to work out.

It helps to think of this as $10\% + 5\% + 2\frac{1}{2}\%$.

To find $17\frac{1}{2}$% of £60:

> 10% of £60 = £6
> 5% of £60 = £3
> $2\frac{1}{2}$% of £60 = £1.50

KEY WORDS

interest   loss
profit   VAT
gain

So $17\frac{1}{2}$% of £60 is £10.50.

£60 with VAT added would be £70.50.

 Find $17\frac{1}{2}$% of three different amounts of money using $10\% + 5\% + 2\frac{1}{2}\%$.

MENTAL ADDITION AND SUBTRACTION

To be comfortable with mental calculations you need to know by heart all the additions and subtractions that make 20. It is also important to be able to work out pairs of numbers that total 1, 10, 100 and 1000 in your head quickly.

- ⦿ Use near multiples of 10 or 100 and adjust the answer.
- ⦿ Use facts you know to work out new facts.
- ⦿ Check a subtraction by addition.
- ⦿ Add up in any order.

Using simple number facts

Use simple number facts you know to work out other facts in your head. You will need to think about zeros and place value as well as the number facts.

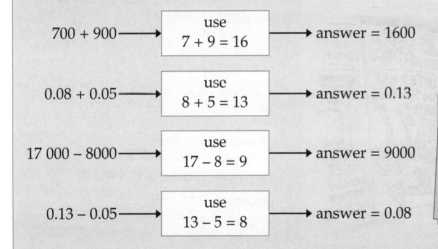

700 + 900 ⟶ use 7 + 9 = 16 ⟶ answer = 1600

0.08 + 0.05 ⟶ use 8 + 5 = 13 ⟶ answer = 0.13

17 000 – 8000 ⟶ use 17 – 8 = 9 ⟶ answer = 9000

0.13 – 0.05 ⟶ use 13 – 5 = 8 ⟶ answer = 0.08

REMEMBER
The place value of the numbers is important. Knowing that 6 + 7 = 13 does not help you answer 0.6 + 0.07.

You can use near multiples of 10, 100 or 1000 to help mental calculation.

REMEMBER
The important part is choosing which near multiple to use and how many you need to adjust your answer by.

750 + 89	→ add on 90 and adjust by 1	→ 839
6500 – 480	→ subtract 500 and adjust by 20	→ 6080
5650 + 3998	→ add on 4000 and adjust by 2	→ 9648
128.5 – 39	→ subtract 40 and adjust by 1	→ 89.5

 Shut your eyes and count back in nines starting from 100.
Shut your eyes and count on in nines from 5.

Mental rules

There are two mathematical rules that help you with mental calculations.

◆ You can add up in any order.

◆ You can check a subtraction answer by addition.

When you have to add two or more numbers the order in which you add them makes no difference to the result. Choose the order you find easiest.

Look for pairs that total 100 first.	Look for pairs that make a multiple of 10.

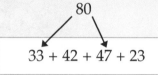

100

60 + 70 + 40 + 90

80

33 + 42 + 47 + 23

> **REMEMBER**
> Addition is the inverse of subtraction.
> Subtraction is the inverse of addition.

More people make mistakes when subtracting than when adding. You can check the result of a subtraction by doing a quick addition as a check.

742 − 377 = 365 ⟶ check by adding 365 + 377 = 742

1.06 − 0.78 = 0.28 ⟶ check by adding 0.28 + 0.78 = 1.06

An important mental skill is knowing what to add to a number to round it up.

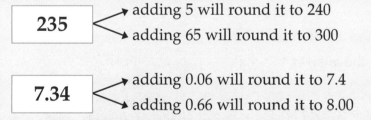

235
- adding 5 will round it to 240
- adding 65 will round it to 300

7.34
- adding 0.06 will round it to 7.4
- adding 0.66 will round it to 8.00

3478
- adding 22 will round it to 3500
- adding 522 will round it to 4000

KEY WORDS

increase
decrease
sum
total
difference
inverse

Write down five sets of three numbers that total 1.

WRITTEN ADDITION AND SUBTRACTION

Most errors made when adding or subtracting are caused by careless mistakes. Setting your work out neatly and checking whether the answer seems sensible will help avoid careless mistakes.

- Line up the numbers when adding or subtracting.
- Check your calculation by another method.

With most calculations you will have to decide the most efficient method for you. What matters is that the answer you get is correct.

✳ Can I calculate these mentally?
✳ Will I have to work it out with pencil and paper?
✳ Should I use a calculator?

Line up the numbers correctly when adding or subtracting.

With whole numbers line up the units digits. Remember the order in which you add does not matter.

2457 + 26 + 156	34 652 – 6486
2457	
156	34652
+ 26	– 6486

With decimals line up the decimal point and make the number of decimal places the same.

12.34 + 0.7 + 3.575	4.2 – 1.375
12.340	4.200
3.575	– 1.375
+ 0.700	

Check addition by adding up in a different order.

Check subtraction by adding the answer to what has been taken away.

If you know this fact: 7456 + 897 = 8353

you should be able to answer these three facts without any more working out:

897 + 7456   8353 – 897   8353 – 7456

REMEMBER
Adding zeros to the ends of a decimal does not alter its value.
0.4 = 0.40 = 0.400

Talk about some different ways of subtracting 25.6 from 1205.
Discuss how the answer can be checked.

Estimating and approximating

When adding and subtracting large numbers or decimals, estimate or approximate the answer to check whether the calculation seems sensible. It does not matter whether you estimate before the calculation or after – it is only a check.

Checks are particularly important if you are using a calculator because it is so easy to enter a number incorrectly.

Knowing what to round each number off to needs some thought. It is no good rounding off to numbers that you cannot **mentally** check.

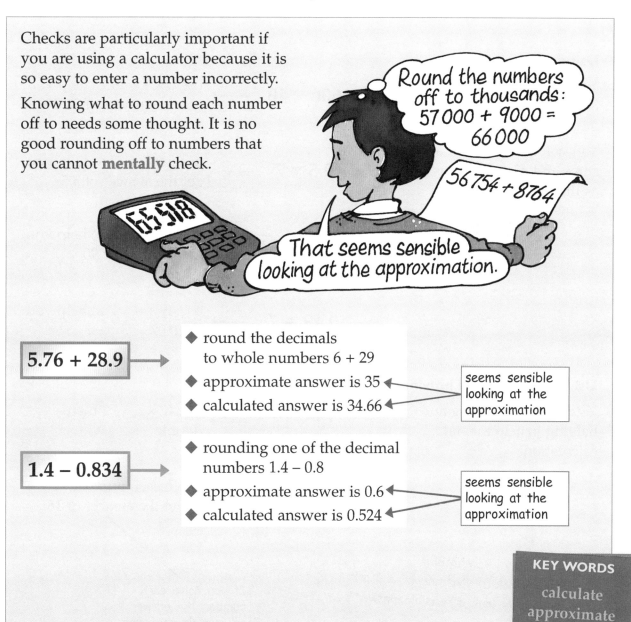

Round the numbers off to thousands:
57 000 + 9000 = 66 000

56 754 + 8764

That seems sensible looking at the approximation.

5.76 + 28.9

- ◆ round the decimals to whole numbers 6 + 29
- ◆ approximate answer is 35
- ◆ calculated answer is 34.66

seems sensible looking at the approximation

1.4 − 0.834

- ◆ rounding one of the decimal numbers 1.4 − 0.8
- ◆ approximate answer is 0.6
- ◆ calculated answer is 0.524

seems sensible looking at the approximation

KEY WORDS

calculate
approximate
round off
inverse

Talk about some different ways of subtracting 0.056 from 0.4.
Discuss how the answer can be checked.

MENTAL MULTIPLICATION AND DIVISION

To be comfortable with mental calculations you need to know by heart all the multiplication and division facts to 10×10.

- Use facts you know to work out new facts.
- Check a division by multiplication.
- Multiply in any order.

Using number facts

You can use simple number facts you know to work out other facts in your head.

You will need to think about zeros and place value as well as the number facts.

| 600×40 | → | use $6 \times 4 = 24$ to help you get the answer of 24 000 |

| 0.5×7 | → | use $5 \times 7 = 35$ to help you get the answer of 3.5 |

| $3600 \div 40$ | → | use $36 \div 4 = 9$ to help you get the answer 90 |

| $0.49 \div 7$ | → | use $49 \div 9 = 7$ to help you get 0.07 |

Using doubling and halving

You can use doubling and halving to help mental calculation.

| 12×12 | → | use $12 \times 6 = 72$ then double |

| $144 \div 8$ | → | halve each number $72 \div 4$ to get the answer of 18 |

REMEMBER
Always look at your answer and ask:
Does this look a sensible answer?

If you halve each number the answer will remain the same.

Discuss different ways of calculating 16×16.

44

Mental rules

There are two mathematical rules that help you with mental calculations.

◆ You can multiply in any order.
◆ You can check an answer to a division by multiplication.

When you have to multiply two or more numbers, the order in which you multiply them makes no difference to the result. Choose the order you find easiest.

More people make mistakes when dividing than when multiplying. So check the result of a division by doing a quick multiplication.

REMEMBER
Multiplication is the inverse of division.
Division is the inverse of multiplication.

$85 \div 5 = 17$ → check by multiplying
$17 \times 5 = 85$

$8.5 \div 5 = 1.7$ → check by multiplying
$1.7 \times 5 = 8.5$

The calculation can be made easy when one of the numbers is a near multiple of 10 or 100.

13×49 → use $(13 \times 50) - 13$
$= 650 - 13$
$= 637$

13×41 → use $(13 \times 40) + 13$
$= 520 + 13$
$= 533$

13×99 → use $(13 \times 100) - 13$
$= 1300 - 13$
$= 1287$

KEY WORDS

product
inverse
double
halve
multiple

Discuss different ways of multiplying 1.2 by 0.5 using mental calculation.

Most errors made when multiplying and dividing are caused by careless mistakes. Using approximation to check whether the answer seems sensible will help avoid this.

- Check your calculation by another method.
- Look at the answer and ask yourself if it seems sensible.
- Approximate to check the answer.

When calculating you will have to decide the most efficient method for you. What matters is that the answer is correct.

Here are some different ways to multiply 86 by 15.

use 15 = 10 + 5	use 15 = 3 × 5
(86 × 10) + (86 × 5)	86 × 5 × 3
860 + 430	430 × 3
= 1290	= 1290

use 86 = 80 + 6 and
15 = 10 + 5

	10	5	
80	100	400	total = 1290
+			
6	60	30	

Here are some different ways to divide 576 by 16.

use halving	use repeated subtraction
288 ÷ 8	16)576
144 ÷ 4	− 160 → 16 × 10
72 ÷ 2	416
= 36	− 160 → 16 × 10
	256
	− 160 → 16 × 10
	96
	− 96 → 16 × 6
	answer = 36

REMEMBER
Check multiplication by multiplying in a different order or using a different method.
Check division by multiplying the quotient by the divisor.

Talk about some different ways of dividing 12.24 by 9.
Discuss how the answer can be checked.

Estimating and approximating

Mental checks are particularly important if you are using a calculator because it is so easy to enter a number incorrectly.

Round off to numbers that you can **mentally** check.

Round the numbers off- say, 300 × 80

approximate answer, 24 000

seems sensible, looking at the approximation.

287 × 77

22.099

33.4 × 4.2

◆ round the decimals 30 × 4
◆ approximate answer is 120
◆ calculated answer is 140.28

seems sensible looking at the approximation

31.5 ÷ 2.1

◆ rounding so numbers can be divided easily 30 ÷ 2
◆ approximate answer is 15
◆ calculated answer is 15.0

matches the approximation

KEY WORDS

calculate
approximate
round off
inverse

Talk about some different ways of dividing 1.44 by 0.4.
Discuss how the answer can be checked.

PROBABILITY AND CHANCE

We use different words to describe the likelihood of something happening:

likely, unlikely, equally likely, likelihood, equal chance, even chance, fifty-fifty chance, fair chance, certain, uncertain, possible, impossible, probable, improbable.

We can work out the mathematical odds of something happening.

- Some events have an equal chance of happening.
- Some events are biased and there is not an even chance.

Some things have an **even chance** of happening.

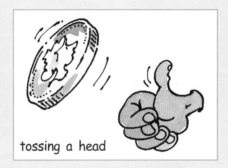

tossing a head

having a baby girl

A **probability scale** shows how likely something is to happen.

Looking at today's weather and reading the forecast, Jamie placed the likelihood of rain on his scale at better than evens.

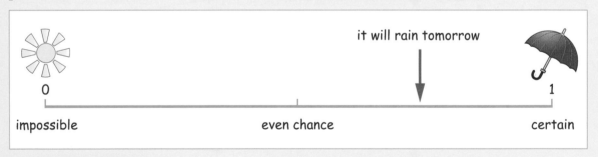

it will rain tomorrow

0		1
impossible	even chance	certain

REMEMBER
These all mean an even or fair chance:
50 : 50, one-in-two, $\frac{1}{2}$, 50%, 0.5.

Think where on the scale these events would be placed.

- ◆ tomorrow will be Sunday
- ◆ dropping an egg will break it
- ◆ winning a world record
- ◆ dropping toast butter side down

Talk about the chances of something definitely happening tomorrow and an evens chance of something happening.

Working out the chance

The chance of something happening can be written as a fraction.

There are six numbers on a dice.
The chance of rolling any one of the numbers is one-in-six or $\frac{1}{6}$.

To work out the chance of an event happening look carefully at all the choices that are available.

What is the chance of picking a red bead out of the bag without looking?

There are 10 beads in the bag and 2 are red.

The chance is 2 in 10 or $\frac{2}{10}$.

Like fractions this is equivalent to $\frac{1}{5}$.

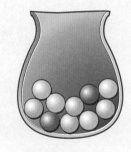

Imagine these 10 playing cards were shuffled and placed face down.

The probability of turning over an even card is $\frac{1}{2}$ because there are 5 out of 10 even cards.

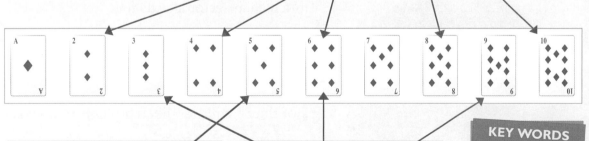

The probability of turning over the 5 is $\frac{1}{10}$ because there is only one 5 in the ten cards.

The probability of turning over multiple of 3 is $\frac{3}{10}$ because 3 out of the 10 cards are multiples of 3.

KEY WORDS

chance
prediction
likelihood
probability

How could you check the prediction that the most common letter used in a story book is the letter e?

PIE CHARTS

A pie chart is a way of showing information. The information looks like slices of a pie. The slices are sectors of a circle. The larger the sector the larger the frequency or amount.

- You can use fractions of a circle to compare the information.
- For accurate comparisons percentages can be used.

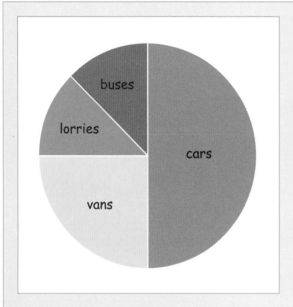

The chart compares the total number of vehicles that passed during one hour.

You can see that $\frac{1}{2}$ the vehicles were cars and $\frac{1}{4}$ were vans.

The buses and lorries were $\frac{1}{8}$ of the total each.

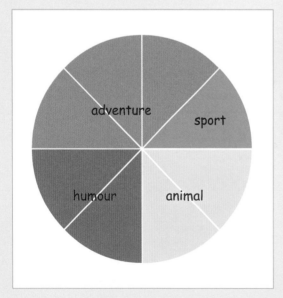

Sometimes the circle is divided into equal slices. This makes it easier to see how much each sector stands for.

$\frac{1}{8}$ of the 80 children liked sport books
$\frac{1}{4}$ of the 80 children liked animal books and $\frac{1}{4}$ liked humorous books.
$\frac{3}{8}$ of the 80 children liked adventure books.

From this information you can work out how many children liked each type of book.

 Look at the traffic survey chart. If 880 vehicles passed in the hour, how many of each type was that?

Reading pie charts

Sometimes the size of each sector is shown as a percentage.
Notice that the percentages must total 100%.

This pie chart shows how a family of four used water during 24 hours.

Just by glancing at the chart you can see how most water was used.

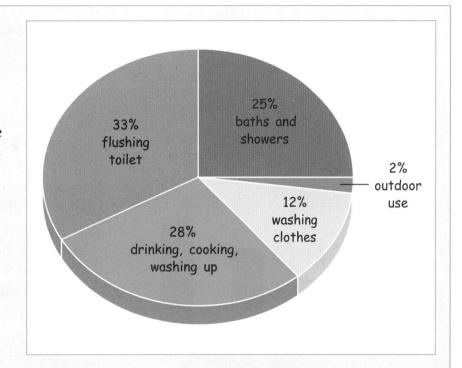

25%
baths and showers

33%
flushing toilet

2%
outdoor use

12%
washing clothes

28%
drinking, cooking, washing up

The water meter showed that they had used 400 litres of water during the day.

From the chart you can work out how many litres each activity used up.

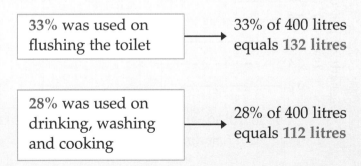

| 33% was used on flushing the toilet | → | 33% of 400 litres equals **132 litres** |

| 28% was used on drinking, washing and cooking | → | 28% of 400 litres equals **112 litres** |

KEY WORDS

pie chart
percentage
sector
comparison

 If one litre is approximately 0.22 gallons, how many gallons were used on each activity?

COLUMN GRAPHS AND BAR CHARTS

The lengths of columns or bars are used to show information. The bar can be so thin that it becomes a stick. The results can be called bar charts, bar graphs, column graphs, bar-line graphs or stick graphs.

- The length of each column or bar represents the value.
- Bars can be horizontal or vertical but columns are always vertical.
- You must check the scale used on the graph or chart.

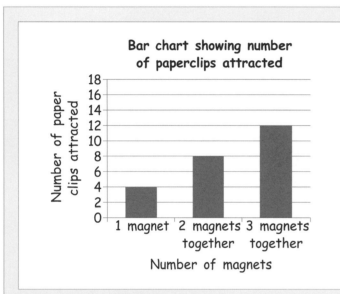

- The x-axis tells you information about the number of magnets used.
- The y-axis has information about the number of clips that were attracted.
- Notice that there is a title and each axis is labelled.
- Look at the scale on the y-axis.
- You can use the graph to predict how many paper clips 4 magnets would attract.

This is a bar-line graph or stick graph showing the results of an experiment conducted with a home-made pendulum.

- Notice the scale used.
- Notice the units of measurements used on each axis.

REMEMBER
The thickness of each bar or column should be the same.

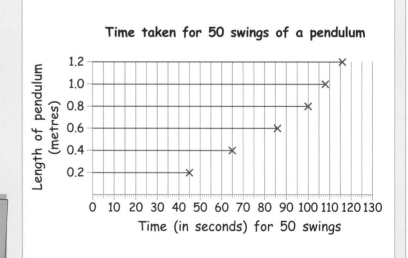

 Try to work out how long it takes a 80 cm pendulum to make 50 swings.

Using column graphs

Sometimes the different columns on a graph each stand for something different.

Blackton School is collecting newspaper vouchers to buy computer software. The column graph shows how they are doing.

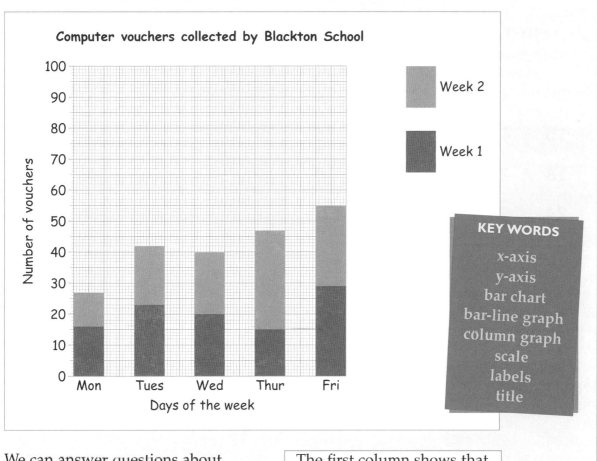

KEY WORDS

x-axis
y-axis
bar chart
bar-line graph
column graph
scale
labels
title

We can answer questions about the total vouchers collected on a particular day of the week ... ⟶ The first column shows that a total of 27 vouchers were collected on two Mondays.

... or about particular days. ⟶ The first Monday collected 16 vouchers and the second Monday collected 11.

 Try to work out the total number of vouchers collected during the second week.

FREQUENCY TABLES AND GRAPHS

A frequency table shows how often an event or quantity occurs.

Information can sometimes be organised into blocks – each block showing a range of numbers.

- Tally marks show how often something occurs.
- The columns of a frequency graph touch each other.

This survey shows the times in minutes people spent in a library.

20	23	17	30	25	20	22	21	25	29
15	19	19	18	25	28	21	22	20	18
18	21	23	26	15	19	22	23	23	24
24	23	20	18	25	22	17	21	16	22

This data can be grouped into a frequency table. The table shows grouped data.

Time in minutes	Tally	Frequency
11-15	II	2
16-20	ΤΗL ΤΗL IIII	14
21-25	ΤΗL ΤΗL ΤΗL ΤΗL	20
26-30	IIII	4

The times have been organised into intervals of 5 minutes. This is called the class interval.

REMEMBER
In grouped data you would not use an interval such as 10-15 followed by 15-20. This would raise the problem of where to place 15.

What are the missing frequencies in the table?
Why do you think tally marks are grouped into blocks of 5?

Reading frequency graphs

Class intervals can be shown on graphs as well as in a frequency table.

This graph shows distances walked during a sponsored charity walk.

Each column is the same thickness. Why do you think this is so?

From the graph you can work things out, such as how many children walked more than 20 km (14 + 12 = 26).

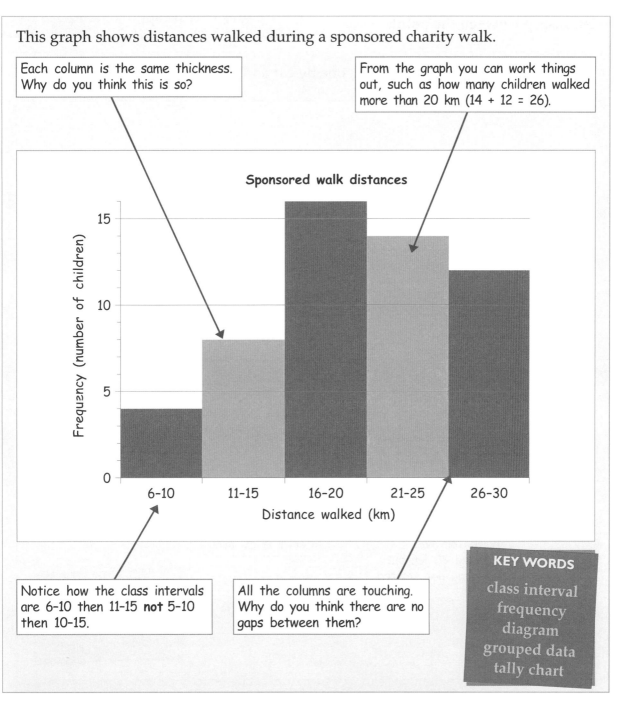

Sponsored walk distances

Notice how the class intervals are 6–10 then 11–15 **not** 5–10 then 10–15.

All the columns are touching. Why do you think there are no gaps between them?

KEY WORDS

class interval
frequency
diagram
grouped data
tally chart

 Calculate the mean average walked by the children.

BROKEN LINE GRAPHS

A broken line graph has points joined together by one or more straight lines. The points are joined to show a **relationship** between the points.

- The plotted points are joined up by straight lines.
- The readings in between the plotted points may be approximate.

The line graph shows two journeys, one by car and one by train.

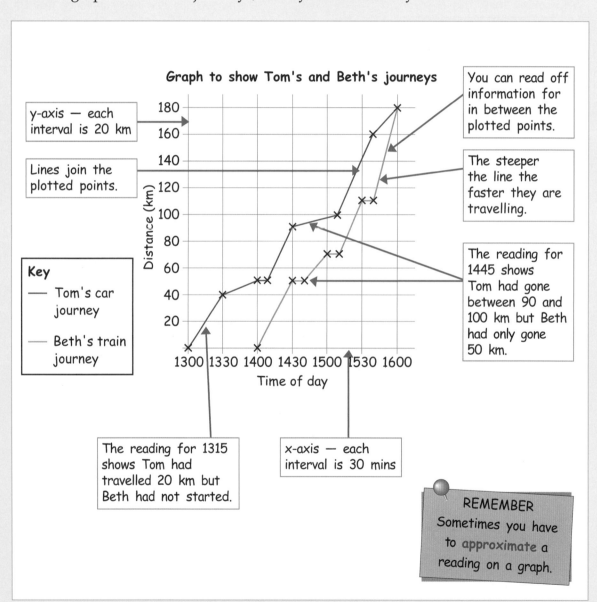

Graph to show Tom's and Beth's journeys

y-axis — each interval is 20 km

Lines join the plotted points.

Key
— Tom's car journey
— Beth's train journey

You can read off information for in between the plotted points.

The steeper the line the faster they are travelling.

The reading for 1445 shows Tom had gone between 90 and 100 km but Beth had only gone 50 km.

The reading for 1315 shows Tom had travelled 20 km but Beth had not started.

x-axis — each interval is 30 mins

REMEMBER
Sometimes you have to approximate a reading on a graph.

Parts of the broken line are horizontal. What do you think that this means?

Temperature graphs

Points can be joined on a temperature graph to show whether the temperature generally goes up or down from one time to another.

The graph shows the mean average temperature taken at the same time each month in some cities.

The points have been joined to show which way the temperature is moving and to compare the different temperatures.

You can see that the January temperature is 37 °C for Alice Springs and -15 °C for Irkutsk. This is a difference of 52 °C.

The hottest temperature reached was 44 °C in Baghdad during August.

Mean average temperature in different cities

Temperature (°C)

50
40
30
20
10
0
-10
-20
-30

Jan Feb Mar Apr May June July Aug Sep Oct Nov Dec
Month

Key
— Alice Springs
— Perth
— Baghdad
— Dunedin
— Tokyo
— Irkutsk

If the line is nearly straight the temperature does not change much from month to month.

Imagine how confusing the graph would look if the points were not joined.

 In which cities did the average temperature drop below 10 °C?

STRAIGHT LINE GRAPHS

On a straight line graph all the plotted points lie in a straight line. A conversion graph is often a straight line graph.

- Conversion graphs are used to change from one unit to another.
- Not all graphs go through the origin.
- The intermediate points of straight line graphs are true.

In a straight-line conversion graph you do not have to plot all the points.

Here is a conversion graph for changing between °F and °C.
Freezing water is 32 °F or 0 °C.
Boiling water is 212 °F or 100 °C.

Plotting these two points makes the **straight line conversion graph**.

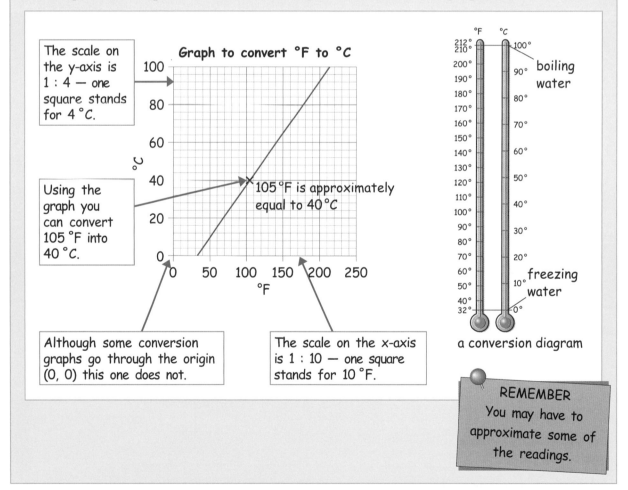

The scale on the y-axis is 1 : 4 — one square stands for 4 °C.

Graph to convert °F to °C

Using the graph you can convert 105 °F into 40 °C.

105 °F is approximately equal to 40 °C

Although some conversion graphs go through the origin (0, 0) this one does not.

The scale on the x-axis is 1 : 10 — one square stands for 10 °F.

a conversion diagram

REMEMBER
You may have to approximate some of the readings.

 Use the graph to convert 80 °F into °C and to convert 80 °C into °F.

When to draw a straight line graph

When you plot several points on a graph and they lie in a straight line you have an important decision to make.

Do you join up the points with a line?

If the intermediate readings are **true** then you **do** join the points.

The results of a science experiment using a newton meter have been plotted and they lie in a straight line.

Graph to show how much a spring stretches as more weight is added

The y-axis has a scale of 1:1 where each square stands for 1 cm.

For each 10 N added the spring gets 4 cm longer.

The results lie almost exactly in a straight line.

They can be joined up because the intermediate readings will be true.

An intermediate reading of 5 N shows that the spring will stretch by 2 cm.

The x-axis has a scale of 1:2 where 1 square stands for 2 N.

KEY WORDS

intermediate
points
axes
labels
scale
convert

 From the information on the graph work out the length of the spring if 120 newtons were added.

AVERAGES

In a range of numbers the average is the typical or middle value.

There are different types of average called mean, median and mode.

- Mean average is the total of the quantities divided by the number of quantities.
- Mode is the amount that appears most often.
- Median is the middle amount.

Time taken to run 100 metres	
Name	Time
Toni	16 secs
Satpal	15 secs
Hannah	19 secs
Fran	19 secs
Will	17 secs

The times in order: 15 16 17 19 19

The **mean** is $(15 + 16 + 17 + 19 + 19) \div 5 = 17.2$ **seconds**.

The **median** is **17 seconds** because it is the middle value.

The **mode** is **19 seconds** because it occurs most often.

The **range** is **4** because that is the difference between the smallest value, 15, and the largest value, 19.

The mean can often be a decimal number.

Children's shoe sizes

The sizes in order:
2 2 2 2 3 4 4 4 4 4 5 5 5 6 6

The **mode** is **size 4** because it the most common.

The **median** is also **size 4** because it is the middle number.

If you tried to calculate the mean you would get 3.8666 ... This isn't sensible because you cannot buy shoes that are size 3.8666.

REMEMBER
When the word average appears on its own it usually means mean average.

 What is the average span size in centimetres of five of your friends or family?

Average results

You might have to interpret a graph to find an average.
The average line can be drawn on the graph to discover
who is over or under the average.

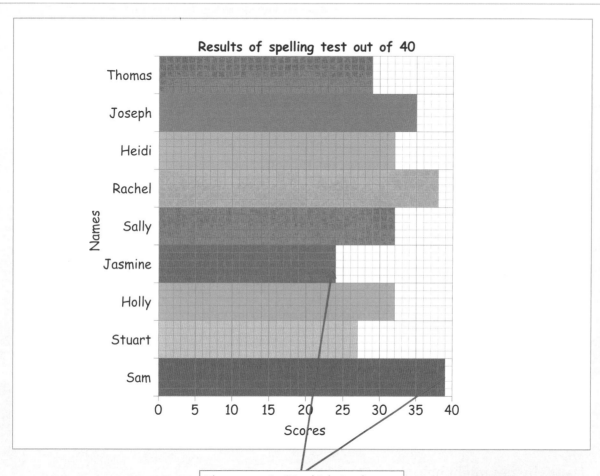

Results of spelling test out of 40

(Names — Scores)

Thomas, Joseph, Heidi, Rachel, Sally, Jasmine, Holly, Stuart, Sam

The range is 15 which is the difference between the highest and lowest scores.

KEY WORDS

average
range
mean
median
mode

The scores in order are: 24, 27, 29, 32, 32, 32, 35, 38, 39.
The median and mode are both 32.

The mean is 288 ÷ 9 which also equals 32.

Look where a line equal to the mean would be drawn on
the graph. You can then see who scored above or below the mean.

 Look at the graph. What was the average number of mistakes?

IMPERIAL UNITS

Measurements can be in
imperial or metric units.

- Imperial units of length include miles, yards, feet and inches.
- Imperial units of weight include tons, pounds and ounces.
- Imperial units of capacity include gallons and pints.

Imperial units of length
12 inches = 1 foot
3 feet = 1 yard
1760 yards = 1 mile

Imperial units of weight/mass
16 ounces= 1 pound
14 pounds = 1 stone
112 pounds = 1 hundredweight
20 hundredweight = 1 ton

Imperial units of capacity
8 pints = 1 gallon

oz is short for ounce
lb is short for pound
cwt is short for hundredweight

Here are some rough metric equivalents to imperial units.

$2\frac{1}{2}$ cm $\approx$ 1 inch	30 g $\approx$ 1 ounce	1 litre $\approx 1\frac{3}{4}$ pints
30 cm $\approx$ 1 foot	1 kg $\approx 2\frac{1}{4}$ pounds	
90 cm $\approx$ 1 yard		$4\frac{1}{2}$ litre $\approx$ 1 gallon
1500 m $\approx$ 1 mile		

These rhymes might help you remember
some equivalent measurements.

*A metre is just three feet three, its longer
than a yard you see.*

*Two and a quarter pounds of jam is round
about 1 kilogram.*

A litre of water's a pint and three quarters.

REMEMBER
Most measuring activities
use approximations.
The sign for approximately
equal to is ≈.

Think about when and where imperial units are still used.

Converting between imperial and metric units

You will see imperial units still being used. Knowing the rough metric equivalent units will help you convert them into metric units.

You will still see distances given in miles.

5 miles ≈ 8 km

To change miles into kilometres divide by 5 then multiply by 8.

$375 \div 5 = 75$ then $75 \times 8 = 600$

So 375 miles ≈ 600 km.

Cricket is played on a pitch that is 22 yards long.

1 yard ≈ 90 cm

So 22 yards ≈ 1980 cm or about 20 metres.

A new baby's weight is often given in pounds.

KEY WORDS

imperial
metric
approximately
round

The baby weighs 8 pounds.

1 pound ≈ 450 g

So 8lb ≈ 3600 g or about $3\frac{1}{2}$ kg.

Using your normal stride work out how many paces you would make in one mile.

READING SCALES

The most common mistake is to read the scale on a measuring instrument wrongly or not accurately enough. You may need to be very accurate. At other times you can round the measurement off.

- Work out the value of the divisions on the measuring instrument.
- Decide whether to measure accurately or approximately.
- Measurements can be metric or imperial.

Working out the value of the divisions on the scale is an important skill.

Here is part of a long tape marked off in mm and cm. Look carefully at how it is numbered.

> The arrow is pointing to a measurement of 27 cm which is 270 mm.

〉 **20** 1 2 3 4 5 6 7 8 9 **30** 1 2 3 4 5 6 7 8 〈

Look at the divisions on the scale.

Each numbered division is 0.1 kg.

Each unnumbered division is half this → 0.05 kg.

> The reading is 0.35 kg.
> 0.35 kg = 350 g

When the pointer is between division marks you will have to approximate the weight.

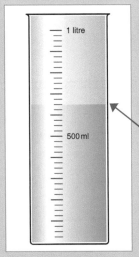

Look at the numbers on the scale. The main units are in 100 ml subdivided into quarters. So each small division is 25 ml.

> The reading is 650 ml.

Think about when you need to measure very accurately indeed such as to the mm, ml or g.

Imperial and metric readings

Some measuring instruments have both metric and imperial units marked on them. You can choose which units you prefer to work in.

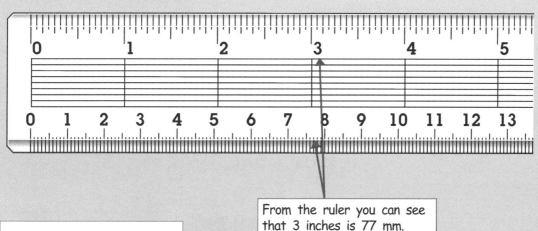

From the ruler you can see that 3 inches is 77 mm.

This scale shows imperial and metric units of capacity.

The litres scale is numbered each 5 l.
Can you work out why each division is worth 1 litre?

The gallons scale is numbered each gallon.
Each division is worth a quarter of a gallon.
A quarter of a gallon is 2 pints.

These bathroom scales show kilograms and pounds.

What is each division on the kg scale worth?

What is each division on the pounds scale worth?

What is the reading in pounds and in kilograms?

Think which instruments might measure in both imperial and metric units.

AREAS

Area is the amount of surface measured in square units such as cm^2, m^2, and km^2.

Complicated shapes can often be broken up into simpler rectangles to work out their area.

- Areas of rectangles are length × breadth.
- Area is measured in square units.

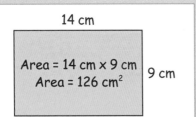

14 cm

Area = 14 cm × 9 cm
Area = 126 cm²

9 cm

A fact to remember is that area of a rectangle or a square is length × breadth.

Areas are always measured in square units:

mm^2, cm^2, m^2, km^2.

1 cm²

Using the area of a rectangle to find the areas of other shapes

- A right-angled triangle is half a rectangle.
- The area of the triangle is half 96 cm² = 48 cm².

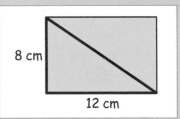

8 cm

12 cm

Using rectangles to find areas of complicated shapes

This shape is a rectangle with a smaller rectangle cut out of it.

- Area of large rectangle 6 cm × 5 cm = 30 cm².
- Area of small rectangle 3 cm × 2 cm = 6 cm².
- Area of shape = 30 cm² – 6 cm² = 24 cm².

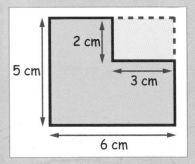

2 cm

5 cm

3 cm

6 cm

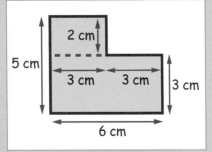

2 cm

5 cm

3 cm 3 cm

3 cm

6 cm

The shape is also two rectangles stuck together.

- Area of large rectangle
  6 cm × 3 cm = 18 cm².
- Area of small rectangle
  2 cm × 3 cm = 6 cm².
- Area of shape =
  18 cm² + 6 cm² = 24 cm².

REMEMBER
Perimeter is the distance all round a shape. It is not measured in square units.

 Think about what could be measured in km^2.

Calculating areas

Sometimes you have to work from plans and diagrams to calculate areas.

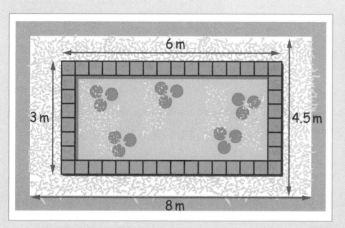

This is sketch of a garden plan.
Problem: *What is the area of the grass?*

Total area is 8 m × 4.5 m = 36 m².
Area of the pond is
6 m × 3 m = 18 m².

The area of the grass is found by subtracting the area of the pond from the total area.

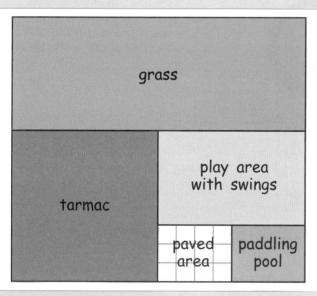

This is a scale drawing.
The scale is 1 cm : 1 m.

The grass on the plan measures 8 cm × 3 cm. The real measurement is 8 m × 3 m. So the area of grass is 24 m².

You can find the surface area of 3D shapes that have rectangular faces.

This cuboid measures 10 cm × 4 cm × 5 cm.

The cuboid has six rectangular faces.

The area of the front and back faces will be 10 cm × 4 cm each.

The area of the two ends will be 4 cm × 5 cm each.

The area of top and bottom faces will be 10 cm × 5 cm each.

 What is the surface area of a 5 cm cube?

TIME

12-hour times use a.m. and p.m. to separate morning from afternoon. 24-hour times number the hours from 01 to 24 and do not use a.m. or p.m.

● 24-hour times use 4 digits. The first two say the hour. The next two say minutes past the hour.

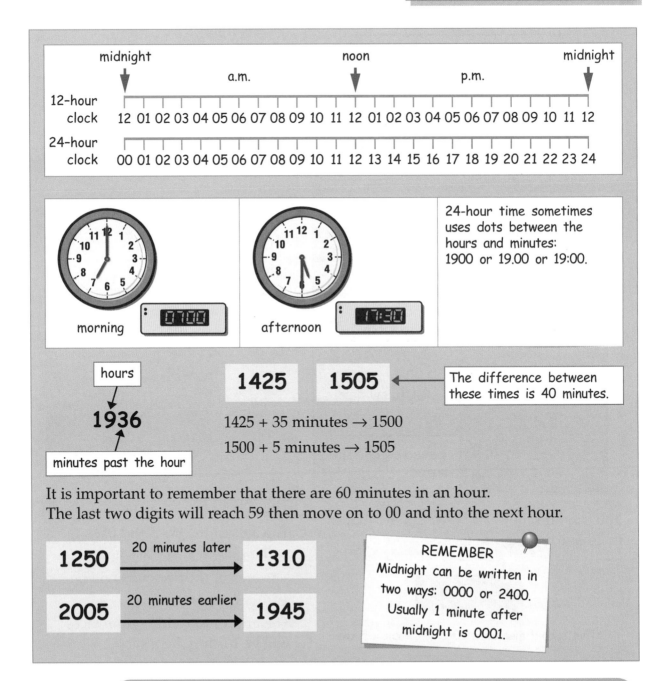

24-hour time sometimes uses dots between the hours and minutes: 1900 or 19.00 or 19:00.

hours

1936

minutes past the hour

1425   **1505** ← The difference between these times is 40 minutes.

1425 + 35 minutes → 1500
1500 + 5 minutes → 1505

It is important to remember that there are 60 minutes in an hour.
The last two digits will reach 59 then move on to 00 and into the next hour.

1250 — 20 minutes later → **1310**

2005 — 20 minutes earlier → **1945**

REMEMBER
Midnight can be written in two ways: 0000 or 2400. Usually 1 minute after midnight is 0001.

What are analogue clocks and watches?

Timetables

Timetables are usually written using 24-hour times. Reading timetables correctly is not always easy.

London–North East England–Scotland

Saturdays										A	B			C		
London Kings Cross	—	—	—	0610	0700	0800	0830	0900	0930	1000	1030	1040	1100	1130	1200	1300
Stevenage	—	—	—	0629	—	0819	—	0919	0949	—	—	—	—	1149	—	1319
Peterborough	—	—	—	0706	0745	0849	0916	0949	1019	1045	1115	1126	1145	1220	1245	1349
Grantham	—	—	—	0725	0804	—					1145			1239	—	
Newark Northgate	—	—	—	0737	0816	—										—
Bedford	—	—	—	0751	—	—	—	—							—	—
Doncaster	—	0610	—	0807	0842	0937	1003	1037	1107	1133	—	—	1232	1313	—	1438
Leeds	—		0710													
York	—	0634	0734	0833	0907	1003	1028	1105	1133	1158	1225	1240	1258	1339	1355	1503
Northallerton	—	0652	—													
Darlington	—	0704	0802	0900	0934	1030	1056	1132	1200	1226	—	1307	1328	1407	—	1530
Durham	—	0722	0820	0918	0952	1048		—	1218		—	1325	—	1425	—	1548
Newcastle	0630	0739	0837	0935	1011	1105	1126	1202	1235	1258	1319	1342	1359	1441	1449	1605
Alnmouth	0658	0811	—	—	—	1133	—	—	1303	—	—	—	—	—	—	1633
Berwick	0720	0833	0922	1021	1057	—	1212	1248	1325	—	—	—	1445	—	—	1656
Dunbar	0747	—	0946	—	—	—	—	1312	—							1720
Edinburgh (arrive)	0809	0918	1015	1109	1142	1239	1259	1338	1413	1428	1451	1512	1432	1611	1625	1748
Edinburgh (depart)	0810	0920	—	1144	—	—	1341	—	—	—	—	1535	—			1751
Motherwell	0856	1006	—	—	1227	—	—	1423	—	—	—	—	1624	—	—	1833
Glasgow Central	0915	1026	—	—	1245	—	—	1443	—	—	—	—	1645	—	—	1852

A: The Flying Scotsman
B: The Northern Lights } Special trains
C: The Highland Chieftan

The timetable shows that:

◆ it takes about 5 hours and 45 minutes to travel from London to Glasgow.

◆ there is a train that starts in Leeds and ends its journey in Edinburgh.

◆ to arrive in Glasgow by 6 o'clock you must catch the 11 o'clock train from London.

Can you work out how long it takes the 0930 train from London to reach Darlington?

KEY WORDS

a.m.
p.m.
midday
midnight
24-hour time
12-hour time

 What do you think the dashes mean on the timetable?

TRIANGLES

A triangle is a polygon that has three straight sides.

Describing the sides of a triangle

Equilateral means equal sided. Each angle is also equal.

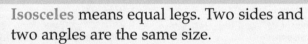

Isosceles means equal legs. Two sides and two angles are the same size.

An isosceles triangle can be right-angled or obtuse.

Scalene means uneven. Each side and each angle is a different size.

A scalene triangle can be right-angled.

Describing the angles of a triangle

Right-angled triangles contain one right angle.

A right-angled triangle can be isosceles.

Acute-angled triangles have each angle less than 90°.

An acute triangle can be isosceles.

Obtuse-angled triangles contain one angle that is greater than 90°.

An obtuse triangle can be isosceles.

What is the size of each angle in an equilateral triangle?
What is the size of each angle in a right-angled isosceles triangle?

Sorting triangles

Carroll diagrams are an excellent way of sorting things to show their properties.

You need to look carefully at the properties in each part of the diagram.

Notice how one part is the 'has the property' and another part is the 'does NOT have the property'. This is what makes the diagram a Carroll diagram.

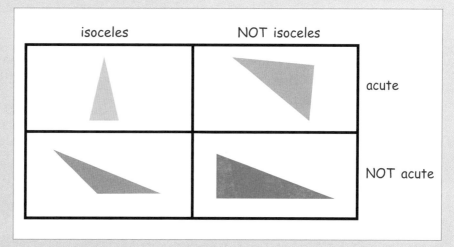

◆ The yellow triangle is isosceles and acute.

◆ The blue triangle is not isosceles but is acute angled.

◆ The pink triangle is isosceles but obtuse not acute.

◆ The orange triangle is not isosceles and not acute, it is right angled.

Think about where you would place other triangles.

> **REMEMBER**
> An equilateral triangle is a very special case of an isosceles triangle. It has three sides and three angles the same size.

Calculating the missing angle

The angles of a triangle total 180°. The missing angle is 30°.

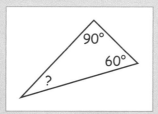

KEY WORDS

acute   equilateral
obtuse   isosceles
right-angled   scalene

QUADRILATERALS

A quadrilateral is a polygon that has four straight sides.

- Square, rectangle, parallelogram, trapezium, rhombus and kite are types of quadrilateral.
- The four angles of a quadrilateral add up to 360°.

Squares and rectangles have four right angles and opposite sides equal.
A square is a special type of rectangle. All its sides are equal.

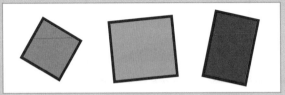

Oblong means longer than wide. There are oblong rectangles and square rectangles.

A kite has two pairs of equal adjacent sides. A special kite has a reflex angle and looks like an arrow head. Kites have one line of symmetry.

Parallelograms have both pairs of opposite sides parallel.

A rhombus is a special parallelogram with adjacent sides equal.

Parallelograms have rotational symmetry.

A trapezium has one pair of parallel sides. It can be right-angled.
A trapezium with two equal sides is called an isosceles trapezium.

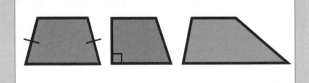

A quadrilateral is any shape that has four sides. As well as the special types it can look like these.

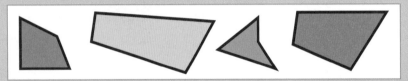

REMEMBER
Shapes can have more than one name.

 Draw diagonals in quadrilaterals. Which diagonals cross at right angles?

Sorting quadrilaterals

Venn diagrams are used to sort things to show their properties.

You need to look carefully at the properties in each part of the diagram.

Notice that the area outside the two loops is used.

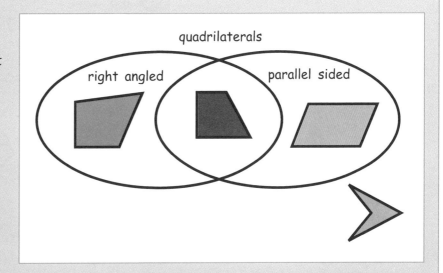

◆ The green kite is right angled but has no parallel sides.
◆ The red trapezium is right angled and has parallel sides.
◆ The yellow parallelogram has parallel sides but no right angles.
◆ The blue quadrilateral has no right angles nor parallel sides.

Think where you would place other quadrilaterals.

Calculating the missing angle

The four angles of a quadrilateral add up to 180°.
The missing angles are 120°.

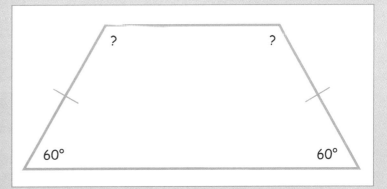

Choose a quadrilateral that is not special to make a tessellating pattern.

POLYGONS

Polygons are 2D shapes that have straight sides. The word polygon means having many angles.

- Polygons can be sorted by the number of sides.
- Polygons can be concave or convex.
- Polygons can be regular or non-regular.

Many polygons have special names according to the number of sides that they have.

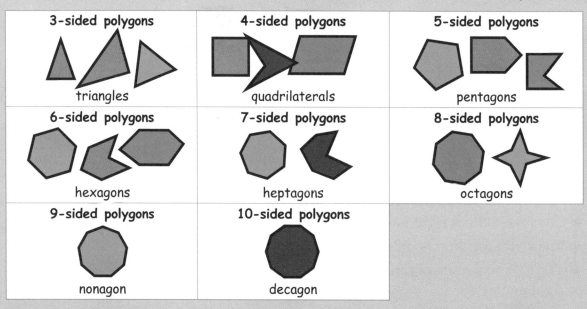

3-sided polygons	4-sided polygons	5-sided polygons
triangles	quadrilaterals	pentagons
6-sided polygons	7-sided polygons	8-sided polygons
hexagons	heptagons	octagons
9-sided polygons	10-sided polygons	
nonagon	decagon	

When all the sides and angles of a polygon are the same size we say that the polygon is regular.

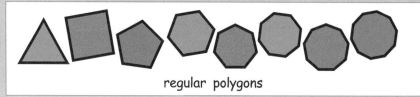

regular polygons

Concave polygons have sides that bend inside the shape.

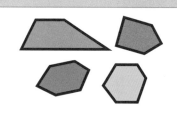

Convex polygons have sides that all bend out.

REMEMBER
A polygon has straight sides not curved.

 How many different 4-sided polygons can you name?

Sorting polygons

Tree diagrams are used to sort things to show their properties. You need to look carefully at the property being used at each branch of the tree.

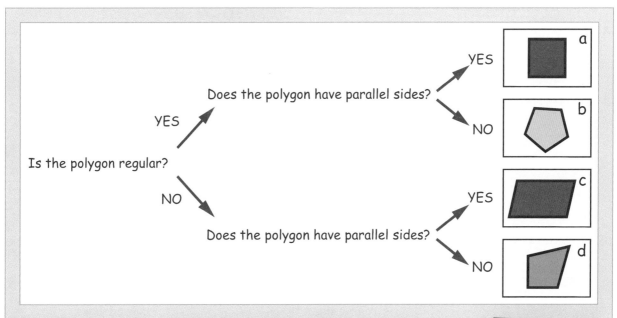

- The red square is regular with parallel sides.
- The yellow pentagon is regular but does not have parallel sides.
- The purple parallelogram is not regular but has parallel sides.
- The green kite is not regular and has no parallel sides.

Think about where other shapes would be sorted.

KEY WORDS

regular
irregular
concave
convex
parallel

A special type of Carroll diagram can be used to sort shapes.

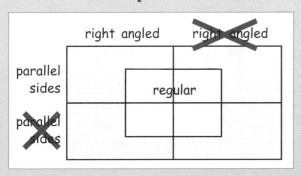

Where do you think these regular polygons would go?

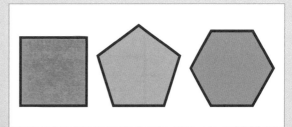

 How many different right-angled polygons can you name?

2D SHAPES

A 2D shape has length and width. These are called the dimensions of the shape.

A 3D shape has length, width and height – it has three dimensions.

All polygons are 2D shapes.

- 2D shapes do not have to be polygons.
- 2D shapes can contain curves.
- Circles and parts of circles are 2D shapes.

Here are some well-known 2D shapes with curves.

A line has one dimension, its length.

Lines can be straight or curved.

straight lines   curved lines

Lines are used to draw 2D shapes.

A circle is a 2D shape. You need to remember what the parts of a circle are called.

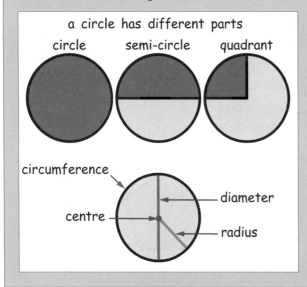

a circle has different parts

circle   semi-circle   quadrant

circumference

centre

diameter

radius

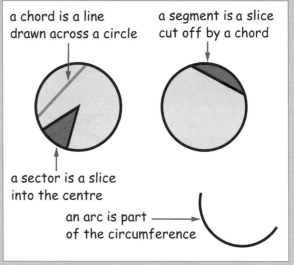

a chord is a line drawn across a circle

a segment is a slice cut off by a chord

a sector is a slice into the centre

an arc is part of the circumference

Draw a pattern with compasses.

Constructions

When you **construct** a 2D shape you draw it very **accurately** with mathematical instruments.

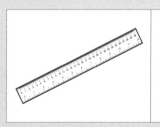  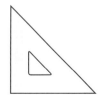 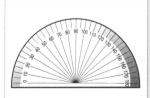

Here is one way to construct a triangle with sides measuring 50 mm, 38 mm and 42 mm.

Step 1

Draw a line 50 mm long.

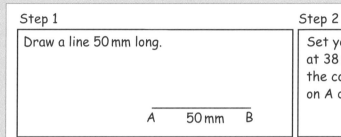

A   50 mm   B

Step 2

Set your compasses at 38 mm and with the compass point on A draw an arc.

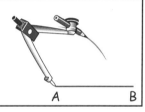

A   B

Step 3

Set your compasses at 42 mm. With the compass point on B draw an arc to intersect the first at C.

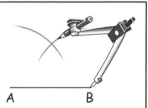

A   B

Step 4

Join AC and BC.

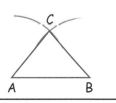

C

A   B

Why do you think we use mm rather than cm when we construct shapes?

Concentric shapes have the same centre.

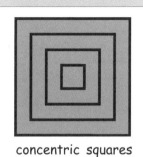

concentric squares   concentric circles

KEY WORDS

construct
intersect
point
straight
curved
concentric
accurate

Construct a rectangle measuring 55 mm by 75 mm.
Talk about the different instruments that could be used to help.

REFLECTIONS

You need to be able to recognise where a shape will be after one or more reflections. A reflection is another name for a flip.

- All shapes can be reflected.
- A reflection depends on where the mirror is placed.

You can reflect any shape in a mirror line. Its reflection with the original shape makes a symmetrical pattern or shape.

non-symmetrical shape

mirror line

reflection

the whole shape now has symmetry

Sometimes the mirror line touches the shape but sometimes it doesn't. This makes a difference to the reflection.

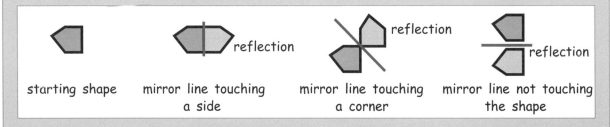

starting shape

mirror line touching a side

reflection

reflection

mirror line touching a corner

reflection

mirror line not touching the shape

You can reflect a shape more than once.

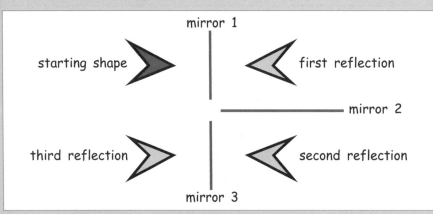

mirror 1

starting shape

first reflection

mirror 2

third reflection

second reflection

mirror 3

REMEMBER
A mirror line acts like a line of symmetry.

 Use a mirror and some shapes. Explore the different polygons you can make by placing the mirror on the edge of the shape.

Reflections on a grid

You can reflect shapes on grids. Notice that the reflection should be the same distance away from the mirror as the original shape.

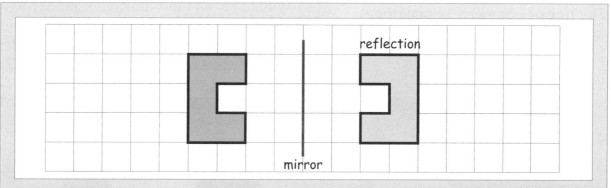

What is the distance of the reflection from the mirror?

You can reflect a shape on grid that has coordinates.

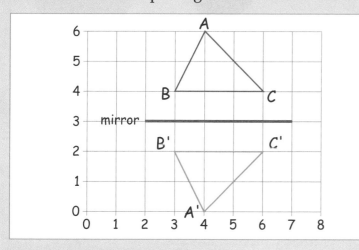

The coordinates of the reflected shape are A' (4,0), B' (3,2), C' (6,2).

KEY WORDS

reflect
flip
reflection
reflective
coordinate

This triangle has been reflected into all four quadrants.

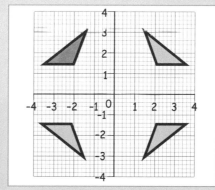

 Draw a shape on squared paper and a sloping mirror line. Sketch the reflection.

LINE SYMMETRY

Some shapes are symmetrical about a line. We say that they have line symmetry or reflective symmetry. The line of symmetry is sometimes called the mirror line.

- Some shapes can have one or more lines of symmetry.
- It is possible for a shape to have line symmetry but not rotational symmetry.
- A line of symmetry can be horizontal, vertical or oblique.

A line of symmetry cuts a shape in half. One half is the reflection of the other half.

These shapes have line symmetry but not rotational symmetry.

Where do you think the line of symmetry is on each picture?

When looking for lines of symmetry on shapes try to find them all. Remember some lines of symmetry can slope.

Regular polygons have more lines of symmetry than non-regular polygons.

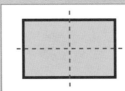 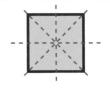

Sometimes the diagonal is a line of symmetry but not always.

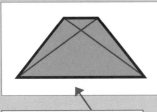 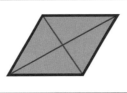   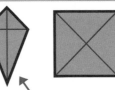

The parallelogram has no lines of symmetry.

The rhombus has 2 diagonals that are lines of symmetry.

The kite has one diagonal as a line of symmetry but one that isn't.

What can you say about the diagonals on the other shapes?

 Draw round some 2D shapes. Show all the lines of symmetry for each shape.

Symmetry patterns

Symmetrical patterns and designs can be drawn on squared paper.

Here are some symmetry patterns made by drawing lines on a 4 × 4 square grid.

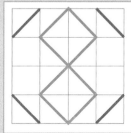 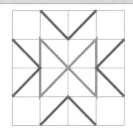 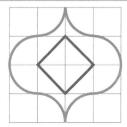 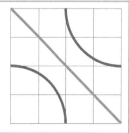

Where do you think the lines of symmetry are?

Here are symmetry patterns made by colouring in squares and part of squares.

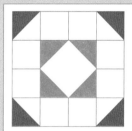 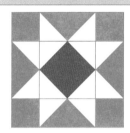 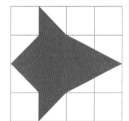 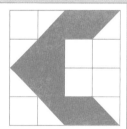

How many lines of symmetry are there for each pattern?

You may be asked to draw a mirror image of a shape or pattern on squared paper. The mirror line is the same as a line of symmetry. The missing half will be a reflection of the shape.

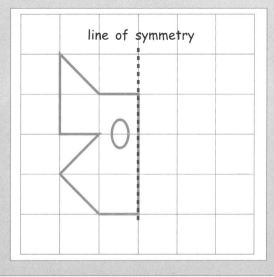

line of symmetry

Use squared paper or a computer program to design your own symmetrical pattern.

ROTATIONAL SYMMETRY

Some shapes are symmetrical about a point. We say that they have rotational symmetry. A shape has rotational symmetry when it will fit into its outline more than once in a complete turn.

- Some shapes can fit into their own outlines several times during a complete turn.
- It is possible for a shape to have rotational symmetry but not line symmetry.
- Some shapes have line and rotational symmetry.

A parallelogram fits into its outline twice in one rotation. It has rotational symmetry. It does not have any lines of symmetry.

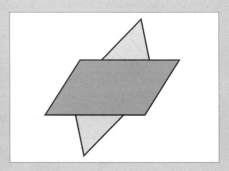

These shapes have rotational symmetry but not line symmetry.

How many times do you think each shape will fit into its outline?

Some shapes can have both line and rotational symmetry.

The point about which you rotate any shape is called the centre of rotation. Can you work out where the centre of rotation is on each shape on this page?

REMEMBER
You can rotate any shape but that does not mean it has rotational symmetry.

 Draw round some polygons and discover which have rotational symmetry.

Rotating and flipping

When you rotate a shape you turn it about a point.
When you flip a shape over you turn it about a line or axis.

This coin has been flipped

This coin has been rotated

Shape 1 will fit into its hole in 4 ways. Twice by rotation, then if you flip it over it will fit twice more.

Shape 7 will fit into its hole in 10 ways. Five times by rotation, then if you flip it over it will fit five times more by rotation.

How many ways do you think the other shapes can be fitted into their holes?

KEY WORDS

symmetrical
rotational symmetry
line symmetry
flip
centre of rotation

 Talk about objects that look the same after a flip and after a rotation.

MOVING SHAPES

You can move a shape from one position to another by:

◆ sliding along – this is called translation.

◆ flipping over – this is called reflection.

◆ turning round – this is called rotation.

- You can move a shape by sliding, rotating or reflecting.
- You can move a shape by combining any of these movements.

A pattern or frieze is being made by moving this tile along in different ways.

Can you describe the rotation the tile has made to create the third pattern?

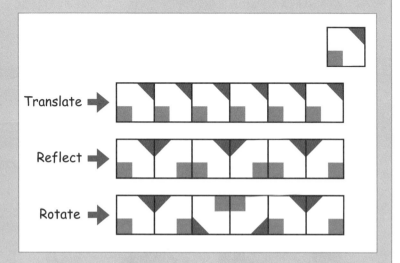

Translate

Reflect

Rotate

Combining slides, reflections and rotations can make tessellation patterns.

Can you describe how the shapes move from one position to another?

REMEMBER
With a regular shape it is sometimes difficult to say which movement has been used. It could have been any one of the three movements.

 Use interesting shapes to make a tessellation.
Describe the movements the shape needs to use to cover a surface.

Moving on a grid

Shapes can be moved about on a grid using coordinates to describe positions. A coordinate grid can have four quadrants. Some of the coordinates will have negative numbers.

You can slide the green triangle to the position of the red triangle.

◆ The coordinates of A have moved from (–3,3) to (2,–1).

◆ The coordinates of B have moved from (–4,1) to (1,–3).

◆ The coordinates of C have moved from (–1,1) to (4,–3).

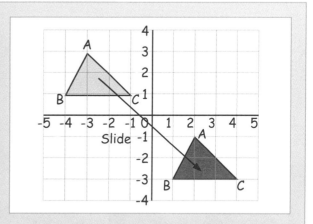

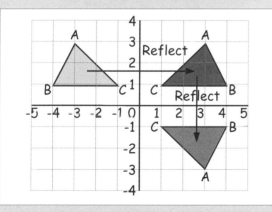

You can reflect the green triangle to the position of the red triangle.

You can then reflect the red triangle to the position of the purple triangle.

KEY WORDS

reflect
rotate
translate
slide

flip
centre of rotation
tessellation

You can rotate the green triangle clockwise to the position of the red triangle. The centre of rotation is 0.

You will notice that it has ended up in the same position as after the two reflections above.

Sometimes you can move to the same position in different ways.

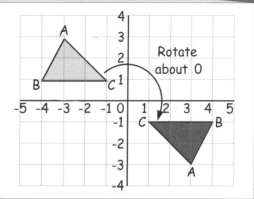

Think about the movements that would move the green triangle into the third quadrant. Which movements would end up flipping the triangle over?

PRISMS

The shape of the polygon ends tells you the name of the prism.

Two special prisms are the cube and cuboid.

> • Prisms have identical ends that are polygons.
> • The cross-section of a prism is always the same shape and size.

Triangular prisms have five faces.

The triangle ends can be any type of triangle.

Slices through the prism will all be the same shape and size.

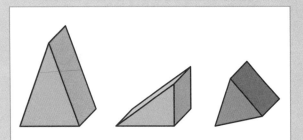

The shape of the ends gives each prism its name.

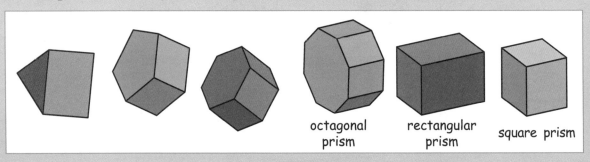

octagonal prism   rectangular prism   square prism

These are special types of prism.

What else are they called?

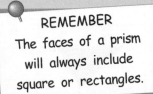

REMEMBER
The faces of a prism will always include square or rectangles.

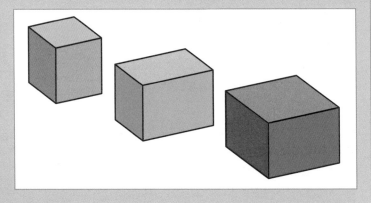

Use interlocking shapes to build different types of prism.
Open out the model to look at the shapes you used.

Nets and frames

The outlines of some 3D shapes can be made from straws or rods to show the frame of a shape. When you open out a 3D shape flat you have made its net.

You can build prisms with straws. The straws are like the edges of the shape.

You can see right through these shapes.
All the edges and vertices are visible.

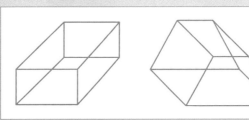

There are 9 edges and 6 vertices or corners.

The net of a shape is what it looks like when it is opened out flat.

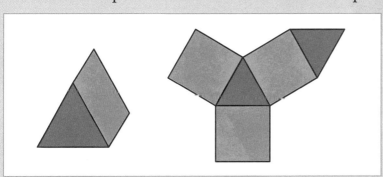

Look at the nets of prisms.

◆ There will be two shapes to match the ends.

◆ The other shapes will always be squares or rectangles.

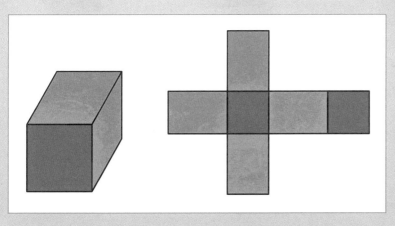

KEY WORDS

net
edges
vertices
faces
prisms

Design the net of a prism that has trapezium ends.

PYRAMIDS AND POLYHEDRA

The shape of the pyramid base tells you the name of the pyramid.

The tetrahedron is a special type of pyramid. The word polyhedron means many faces.

- Pyramids have a polygon base and triangle sides.
- Polyhedra are 3D shapes with polygon faces.

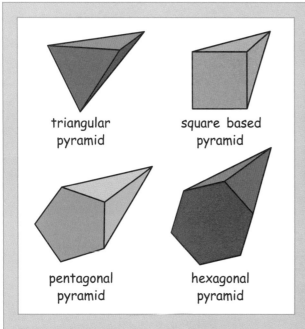

triangular pyramid

square based pyramid

pentagonal pyramid

hexagonal pyramid

Another name for the triangular pyramid is the tetrahedron. Each of the four faces is a triangle.

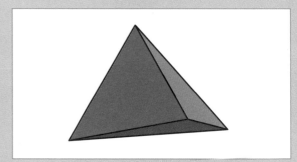

A polyhedron is any 3D shape that has faces, edges and vertices. Some polyhedra have special names such as cube, cuboid, prism and pyramid.

When each face is an identical regular polygon, the shape is a regular polyhedron.

Look at the faces on these regular polyhedra.

REMEMBER
All the faces of a polyhedron are flat.

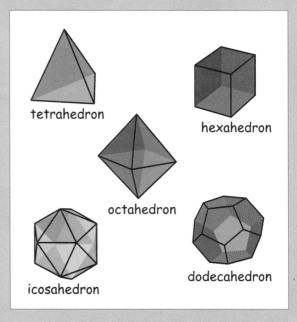

tetrahedron

hexahedron

octahedron

dodecahedron

icosahedron

 Use interlocking shapes to build different types of polyhedra. Which of your models has parallel faces?

Views of polyhedra

When you look at a solid shape from the top, side and front you get different views of the same shape. From these three views it should be possible to make the shape.

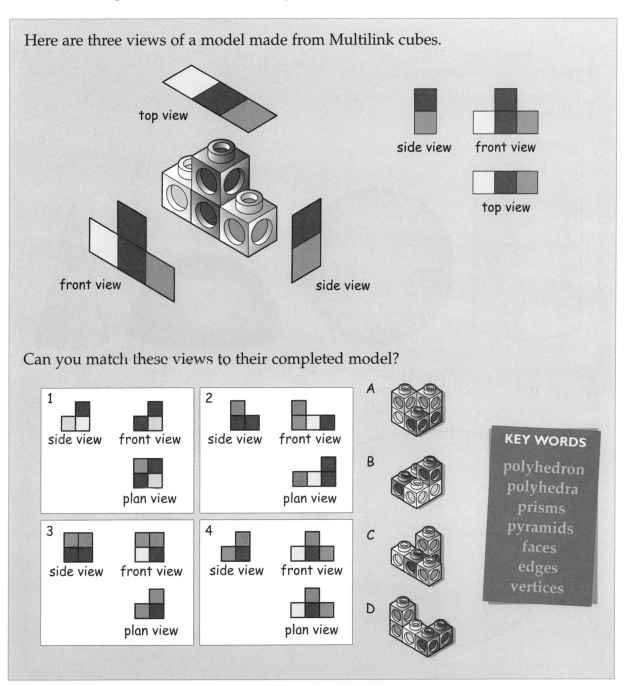

Here are three views of a model made from Multilink cubes.

top view

side view   front view

top view

front view   side view

Can you match these views to their completed model?

1
side view   front view
plan view

2
side view   front view
plan view

3
side view   front view
plan view

4
side view   front view
plan view

A

B

C

D

Make a 'secret' model from interlocking cubes. Give instructions to some partners so that they make an exact copy of the unseen model.

3D SHAPES

A 3D shape has length, width and height. These are called the dimensions of a shape.

A 2D shape has only two dimensions – length and width.

- 3D shapes can have curved faces.
- 3D shapes include all the polyhedra.

Here are some well-known 3D shapes with curves.

Can you name each of these 3D shapes?

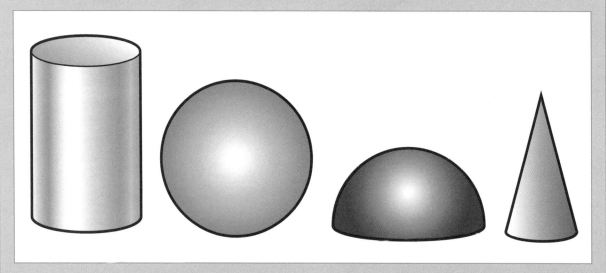

A shape like an egg is called an ovoid.

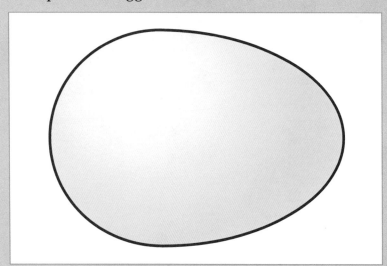

> **REMEMBER**
> 3D shapes can have several names. A cube is a: hexahedron, square prism, polyhedron, regular solid, 3D shape.

 Discuss which 3D shapes have a cross section that is always the same and which have cross sections that change.

Cylinders and pi

You can use cylinders to work out the value of pi, π. When measuring curves you often have to try different ways.

To work out the value of pi, π, you need to find the diameter of some cylinders.

Put the cylinder between two blocks of wood and measure the distance apart.

Use bow calipers...

or sliding calipers

Then measure the circumference of each cylinder.

Mark and roll the cylinder

MARK

START   MEASURE   FINISH

Measure with string

If you divide each diameter into each circumference the answer is about 3, which is the value of pi, π.

$$\text{pi } (\pi) = \frac{\text{circumference}}{\text{diameter}}$$

KEY WORDS

cylinder   circumference
cone   diameter
sphere   pi
hemisphere   π

**Measure some circumferences and diameters.
See if you can calculate pi from them.**

ANGLES

An angle is an amount of turn or the size of a corner on a shape.

Angles can be right-angled, acute, obtuse or reflex.

- An angle is an amount of turn measured in degrees (°).
- Protractors are used to measure angles.
- The three angles in a triangle total 180°.

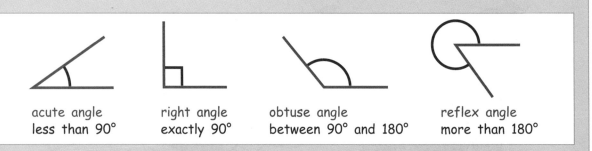

acute angle
less than 90°

right angle
exactly 90°

obtuse angle
between 90° and 180°

reflex angle
more than 180°

About right angles

One right angle is a quarter turn.

Two right angles is a half turn or a straight angle.

Three right angles is a three-quarter turn

Four right angles is a complete turn.

Right-angled shapes contain angles of 90°.

A protractor is used to measure angles.

Before measuring, decide whether the angle is more or less than 90°. This will stop you reading the wrong number on the protractor.

Some protractors are semicircles and measure up to 180°.

Some protractors are whole circles and measure up to 360°.

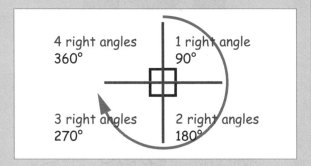

4 right angles
360°

1 right angle
90°

3 right angles
270°

2 right angles
180°

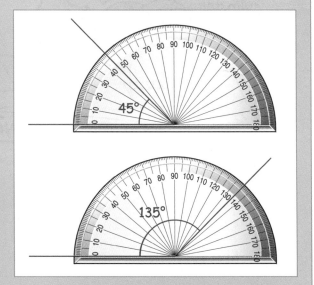

45°

135°

Use a protractor to measure some angles on 2D shapes.

Working with angles

The three angles of a triangle add up to 180°. Here is one way of showing this.

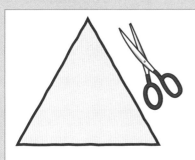

Cut out any triangle.

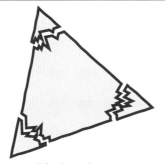

Rip off the three corners.

Arrange the three corners to make a straight angle of 180°.

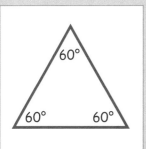

In an equilateral triangle each angle is the same size. Each one must be 60°.

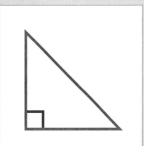

This triangle is right angled and isosceles. Can you work out how large each angle is?

Here is way to bisect an angle. When you bisect something you cut it in half.

draw an angle

draw an arc

draw a second arc

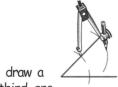

draw a third arc

draw a fourth arc to intersect the third arc

join the intersecting arcs to the vertex

KEY WORDS

angle
degrees
protractor
acute
obtuse
reflex
intersect
bisect
arc

Draw perpendicular lines. Check that they meet at 90°.
Discuss how the lines can be drawn accurately.

DIRECTIONS

Directions such as left and right can be misunderstood. They depend upon which way you are facing.

Directions using compass points are useful because north always faces the same direction.

Bearings use degrees of turn and are an accurate way of finding directions.

- You can describe direction using left, right, clockwise and anticlockwise.
- You can give directions using the compass points.
- You can measure directions using bearings.

Here are the 4 points of the compass. They are called the cardinal points.

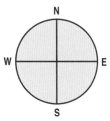

90° of turn between each direction

Here are the 8 points of the compass.

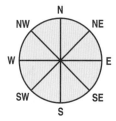

45° of turn between each direction

Here are the 16 points of the compass.

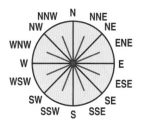

$22\frac{1}{2}$ ° of turn between each direction

Bearings measure the direction from north turning in a clockwise direction. They are measured in degrees.

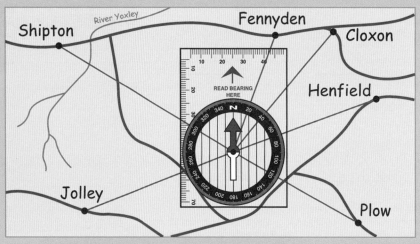

REMEMBER
Bearings always use 3 digits. Bearings less than 99° have a zero in front of them.

The bearing of Henfield is 070°. The bearing of Jolley is 250°. The bearing of Shipton is 300°. What are the bearings of the other towns?

 Use a compass to find directions of different places around you.

Directions on a map

You can use the scale on a map and bearings to measure distances between places quite accurately.

The treasure map shows where the treasure is hidden. Look at the scale of the map and the bearings. There is enough information to find the treasure. You can estimate the angles or use a protractor to help.

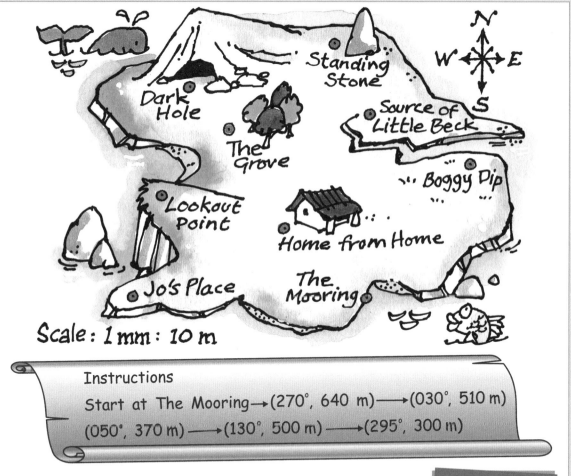

Scale: 1 mm : 10 m

Instructions

Start at The Mooring → (270°, 640 m) → (030°, 510 m)
(050°, 370 m) → (130°, 500 m) → (295°, 300 m)

The first bearing takes you to Jo's Place.
From here the second bearing takes you to The Grove.
The third bearing takes you to Standing Stone.
Can you work out the next two bearings and find where the treasure is buried?

KEY WORDS

compass point
bearing
direction
scale

Make up your own treasure map with bearings and scale.
Ask a friend to find the treasure.

GLOSSARY

average The typical or middle number of a range of numbers. The different types of average are the median, mean and mode.

decimal Numbers based on 10.

denominator The bottom number in a fraction.

equivalent Things that are worth the same. Simplifying a fraction by cancelling makes an equivalent fraction.

factor A number that will divide exactly into another number.

imperial Measurements not based on 10, such as miles, yards, ounces and gallons.

improper fraction A fraction where the numerator is larger than the denominator.

integer A whole number or zero.

inverse The opposite of something.

mean The mean average is the total of a group of numbers divided by how many numbers there are in the group.

median The middle number in a group of numbers arranged in order.

mixed number A number made of an integer and a fraction.

mode The number which appears most often in a group of numbers.

numerator The top number in a fraction.

percentage A fraction out of 100. Another way of showing hundredths. They are written with a percentage sign, %.

polygon The general name for 2D shapes with straight sides. They include squares, pentagons and triangles.

polyhedron The general name for 3D shapes that have flat faces. They include pyramids and cubes.

prime number A number that is only divisible by itself and 1.

probability The chance or likelihood that something will or will not happen, such as rolling a 6 on a dice.

quotient The number that is made by a division, for example the quotient from the division of $7 \div 3$ is $2\frac{1}{3}$.

range The difference between the highest and lowest numbers in a group of numbers arranged in order.

ratio This compares two or more quantities. If a ratio is 2 : 1, then something is twice as large as something else.

recurring decimal A decimal that goes on and on, like 0.333333333.... They are usually rounded to two or three decimal places, in this case 0.33.

reflection A flip across a mirror line.

sequence A set of numbers which go up or down in similar steps, either of the same size or changing in the same way.

symmetry Shapes may have line symmetry, where one side of the shape could be reflected on the line to give the shape on the other side. Shapes may also have point symmetry, where the shape can be rotated around a point to fit into its own outline.

tessellation Creating a pattern by translating, reflecting and rotating a shape to fill a space without leaving gaps or overlapping.

vertices The corners of a shape.

vulgar fraction A fraction where the numerator is less than the denominator.